W9-DHU-900

OUTCOMES-BASED ACADEMIC AND CO-CURRICULAR PROGRAM REVIEW

OUTCOMES-BASED

ACADEMIC AND

CO-CURRICULAR

PROGRAM REVIEW

A Compilation of Institutional Good Practices

Marilee J. Bresciani

Foreword by Ralph Wolff

STERLING, VIRGINIA

65644320

Sty/us

COPYRIGHT © 2006 BY
STYLUS PUBLISHING, LLC

Published by Stylus Publishing, LLC
22883 Quicksilver Drive
Sterling, Virginia 20166-2102

Library of Congress Cataloging-in-Publication Data
Bresciani, Marilee J.
  Outcomes-based academic and co-curricular program review : a compilation of institutional good practices / Marilee J. Bresciani ; foreword by Ralph Wolff.—1st ed.
    p. cm.
  Includes bibliographical references.
  ISBN 1-57922-140-8 (hardcover : alk. paper)—
  ISBN 1-57922-141-6 (pbk. : alk. paper)
    1. Educational tests and measurements—United States. 2. Competency based education—United States. 3. College teaching—United States.
  4. Education, Higher—United States. I. Title.
    LB3051.B693 2006
    378.1'66—dc22   2006009490

ISBN: 1-57922-140-8 (cloth)/13-digit 978-1-57922-140-9

ISBN: 1-57922-141-6 (paper)/13-digit 978-1-57922-141-6

Printed in the United States of America

All first editions printed on acid-free paper
that meets the American National Standards Institute
Z39-48 Standard.

Bulk Purchases

Quantity discounts are available for use in workshops and for staff development.
Call 1-800-232-0223

First Edition, 2006

10   9   8   7   6   5   4   3   2   1

This book is dedicated to all the faculty, staff, and students who care about student learning and development—who have made their institutions role models for good practice in outcomes-based assessment program review and to all those who will. I have truly been inspired by your concern and commitment to student-centered learning, and may you continue to "measure what you value, rather than valuing what you can measure."

CONTENTS

FOREWORD

This is a much-needed book for all institutions of higher education. Ten years ago, or even five, outcomes assessment and program review were both largely misunderstood, rarely linked, and neither were well embedded in institutional practice. Growing concerns about the quality of American higher education, combined with concerns over our country's competitiveness in an increasingly global marketplace, have led to calls for greater accountability and transparency in the performance of all colleges and universities. Since a higher education degree is now considered to be essential for a productive workforce, a large spotlight is being shone on whether America's institutions of higher education can articulate learning outcomes for the twenty-first century and demonstrate that these outcomes are being achieved.

Recently published results from the administration of the National Assessment of Adult Literacy found that the majority of college graduates (and even those with graduate degrees) could not perform at a proficient level such basic skills as reading a map, working with a prose text, or performing basic math computations. Similar results were found when the same tests were administered to seniors at a wide range of two-year and four-year colleges and universities.

Concerns also exist about the retention and graduation rates of today's students. As of the time of publication, only 54 percent of students will graduate in six years, and the graduation rates of underrepresented minorities are significantly lower. With the majority of today's graduates attending more than one institution, there is concern that students will get lost, and that institutions, and particular disciplines, will seek to serve only the best students, weeding out the rest. It is well understood that our country cannot afford such an approach, and that we need to ensure that *all* students are served well and provided the support to graduate once they have been admitted.

Some in the public policy arena call for a mandatory system of national or statewide testing, so that the results of each institution's graduates can be published and compared, creating, it is assumed, a public incentive for improvement. This is a large part of the foundation underlying No Child Left Behind. Many feel that a similar approach should be extended to higher education.

The development of new tests, such as the Collegiate Learning Assessment (CLA), and the availability of other tests from ACT and ETS, have given rise to the belief by some that we now at are a point where tests are reliable enough to be used as a comparative benchmark on a statewide or national basis. The National Center for Public Policy in Higher Education has already undertaken a pilot test in five states using test results and other indicators to measure and then compare state performance on a statewide, rather than institutional, basis.

Institutions of higher education, however, prefer to be seen and understood in the context of their own missions, and the success of American higher education is frequently described as being due not only to the significant number of institutions (more than 3,900) but also to the rich mosaic of institutional types, from elite research universities and liberal arts colleges, to community colleges and comprehensive public universities, to faith-based institutions and special-purpose institutions (such as art, music, and architecture). Higher education would like to be judged relative to the success of each institution achieving its mission.

Historically, accreditation has served as one of the principal quality assurance agents in this system. It has focused on each institution's mission and evaluated whether that mission is being achieved. Over the past decade, however, accrediting agencies have shifted their focus to include attention to results, and now all accrediting agencies require institutions to identify and assess student-learning outcomes as a central part of the accrediting process. Several of the regional accrediting agencies, such as the Senior College Commission of the Western Association and the Academic Quality Improvement Program (AQIP) model of the Higher Learning Commission of North Central, have transformed the accrediting process to focus on student and organizational learning. ABET, Inc., has similarly moved to create an outcomes-based accreditation process for all engineering programs.

What is apparent from the national dialogue on higher education today, and the significant changes in accreditation practice, is that institutions will need to articulate learning outcomes for the baccalaureate degree as a whole and for each program or major. Legislation has been suggested to have these outcomes made public on each institution's website, along with indicators, outcomes, and performance data with respect to the outcomes appropriate to the institution's mission. While not yet adopted, this proposal reflects a trend that is likely to continue for the foreseeable future. Another proposal calls for each institution to identify benchmarks for comparisons for each institution and program similar in type or mission, and for institutions and programs to actively seek out "best practices" from other institutions in the United States or beyond.

An equivalent concern exists about improving retention and graduation rates, and there are calls for developing a national student identifying and tracking system to obtain more accurate data on student progress through different institutions. New websites promote comparative data as well as best practices for retention, such as those of The Education Trust and of Documenting Effective Educational Practice (DEEP) briefs, published by the National Survey for Student Engagement. From available data there are serious concerns not only over significantly different graduation rates for underrepresented minorities, but also over the production of those graduating in the science, technology, engineering, and math (STEM) disciplines. Retention and graduation rates, therefore, need to be developed and analyzed not only in the context of the institution as a whole, but also for each department and program.

America's institutions of higher education are capable of responding to these challenges but to do so, far more will be required than the traditional focus of worrying most about who gets in (selectivity), the institution's ranking in *U.S.News and World Report* (reputation), and the comparative size of resource measures, whether for endowment, library, or technology. Even student satisfaction survey results will not be sufficient to respond to these concerns.

For most faculty and staff, it is easier and more motivating to focus on the performance of the specific unit where each person works than on institutionwide goals and outcomes. While such focus is necessary, it is the responsibility of each unit within any institution, regardless of its mission, to ensure that it is connected to the educational (and learning) mission of the institution and is actively reviewing evidence of its performance to improve.

It is in this context that *Outcomes-Based Academic and Co-curricular Program Review* provides a wealth of information that can be used at the program and departmental level to address these concerns. Building on the practices of institutions with substantial experience (and success) with program review and assessment, it provides an enormously useful compilation of the steps institutions need to undertake for effective outcomes-based program review, and the elements within each of these steps that should be considered. The book also shows how to link outcomes-based assessment with program review, since these two activities, when undertaken at all, are often decoupled. As a result, the book is a resource that can be referred to time and again as different issues arise.

Program review can be an effective process to respond to the external concerns described above, while at the same time providing much needed information for improvement of quality and the effectiveness of each program or unit. It is an essential process to ensure the currency and effectiveness of all programs—academic and nonacademic. It should be central to any institution's quality assurance process. Yet not all institutions engage in periodic program review, and even fewer implement program review effectively across all units. One of the key reasons is that administrators and faculty alike too often do not understand the purpose and value of program review. *Outcomes-Based Academic and Co-curricular Program Review* responds to this need by providing the most comprehensive and usable treatise on program review available today.

If done appropriately, program review provides a singularly effective way of addressing both the need for internal improvement and external accountability. It allows each program or unit to review itself in light of its outcomes and in relation to the institution's mission and goals. Such outcomes information can be used by the program and the institution to document learning results and program improvements. In turn, they can be part of a program's or institutions external accountability report. Equally, if not more important, however, outcomes-based program review can assist each department or unit to determine the extent to which it is successful in serving a wide range of students; identify indicators of learning effectiveness at the program, not just the course level; and assist the program or unit in assessing how well it is contributing to general education or institutional goals and objectives.

Outcomes-based program review can also be used to assess issues of retention and graduation rates, since these are often best considered at the departmental level. In light of each academic unit's performance, the role of support services can also be reviewed in terms of their contributions to addressing retention and graduation.

The Senior College Commission of Western Association of Schools and Colleges (WASC), one of seven regional accreditors, has required program review for many years, and in its 2001 Standards of Accreditation expanded that requirement so that all program reviews are now expected to include consideration of learning effectiveness and the achievement of the program's learning outcomes. Other regional and specialized accreditors now hold similar expectations as well.

Our experience has demonstrated that program review is uniquely valuable. It allows faculty and staff of programs and nonacademic units to focus on their own units, which they typically care about the most. When taken seriously, such reviews have led to discussions that are much needed within the program or unit about important issues, and external reviewers can bring insights and significant recommendations for improvement.

Traditionally, however, program reviews focus on curriculum or resource needs, such as the need for additional courses, faculty, or library holdings. Inevitably, these recommendations all call for more resources. But it is not always clear that the addition of new courses or faculty will lead to greater learning effectiveness. Such reviews typically have not addressed the multiple dimensions of effectiveness of the program or unit, such as retention, graduation rates, and achievement of learning or other outcomes.

Linking program review with outcomes assessment provides an opportunity to address key indicators of performance in new and fresh ways. Program faculty and staff, even students, find great value in clarifying learning outcomes and determining the most effective ways of assessing their achievements within the context of the department or institution's mission. Crosscutting criteria can also be identified, along with cognitive outcomes, such as attention to and learning results in such areas as ethics, value or spiritual formation, appreciation of diversity or multiple frameworks, and so on. By developing a framework for inquiry, useful data can be generated that faculty, staff, and students can then analyze—perhaps the most important part. Too often data is not developed or presented in ways useful for those needing to analyze and apply it, and a key part of any outcomes-based program review process is developing, at the outset, an awareness of what data will be generated and how it will be presented and then actually working with the data to see how to apply it to make improvements.

Outcomes-Based Academic and Co-curricular Program Review also provides information on the challenges institutions have faced, and how they addressed them. Initiating any process as important as this will encounter expected and unexpected challenges, and the experience of those institutions in the book, and how they addressed their challenges, serves as a guide for all.

This book is worth reading, but even more important, it is worth *using*. The author is to be commended for preparing such a timely and needed resource for all of us in higher education to use.

Ralph A. Wolff
President and Executive Director
Accrediting Commission for Senior Colleges and Universities
Western Association of Schools and Colleges

ACKNOWLEDGMENTS

I wish to acknowledge the contributions of the good practice institutions for their participation in this study. Their assistance in defining what constitutes good practice and their generous sharing of their own good practice examples are what make this book informative. I wish that I could have placed all of their wonderful examples in this book, but since we had to cut the first draft in half to make it affordable to print and purchase, many of their original contributions had to be scaled down. I hope the readers of this book are able to follow up with these institutions and are able to refer to http://styluspub.com/resources/outcomes-basedprogramreview.aspx to learn more about their very fine practices. In particular, I wish to acknowledge the following scholars:

Alverno College
William H. Rickards, Glen Rogers, and Marcia Mentkowski

Azusa Pacific University
Bonnie Hedlund

California State University, Monterey Bay
Diane Cordero de Noriega, Betty McEady, Richard Harris, Marsha Moroh, Joe Larkin, Octavio Villalpando, John Laughton, Judith White, Herb Martin, Suzanne Worcester, and Josina Makau

California State University, Sacramento
Linda Buckley

Hampden–Sydney College
Elizabeth J. Deis and Earl Fleck

Indiana University–Purdue University Indianapolis (IUPUI)
Trudy W. Banta and Karen Black

Isothermal Community College
Nancy Womack

John Carroll University
Megan Gardner (currently at University of Akron)

Keystone College
Sherry Strain

Maryland Community Colleges
Cindy Peterka, Rashida H. Govan, Rich Haney, and Charlene Dukes

Miami University
Jerry Stillwater

New Jersey City University
Sandra Bloomberg, Arthur Kramer, Joanne Bruno, Maria Lynn Malik, and Muriel Rand

North Carolina State University
John Ambrose, Chris Anson, Arnold Bell, Susan Blanchard, Michael Carter, Thomas Conway, Allen DuPont, Candace Goode-Vic, Karen Helm, Marian McCord, Jon Rust, Ephraim Schechter, Joni Spurlin, and John Tector

Oregon State University
Rebecca A. Sanderson, Larry Roper, and Eric Hansen

Sinclair Community College
Sue Merrell

Texas A&M University
Valerie Balester, Becky Carr, Bryan Cole, John Fackler, Charles Farnsworth, Matt Fuller, Claude Gibson, Martyn Gunn, Walter Haisler, Jimmie Killingsworth, Debbie Kochevar, Marty Loudder, Marti Marberry,

Peter McIntyre, Paul Meyer, Sandi Osters, Linda Parrish, Bill Perry, David Prior, Nancy Simpson, Doug Slack, Nancy Small, Beth Tebeaux, and Paul Wellman

Truman State University

Sue Pieper, Daniel Hite, Don Kangas, Jeanne Mitchell, Janet Gooch, and Paula Cochran

United States Naval Academy

Peter Gray

University of Wisconsin at Whitewater

Richard Telfer

Additional details about the good practice institutions and their websites can be found in Appendix A.

I also wish to acknowledge the help of three Texas A&M University graduate students: Catherine Tonner, Natasha Croom, and Keith Wycliffe. As a part of their graduate work, Natasha and Keith assisted with the development and administration of the good practice survey. Catherine assisted with clarifications of references and appendices. Assessment professional Michelle Rosowsky of Texas A&M University, formerly of Oregon State University, assisted with additional research on the good practice institutions for the completion of the book and provided content editing. Thanks also to undergraduate researcher Courtney Wall and professional colleague Matt Fuller, both of Texas A&M University, for additional editing and proofing.

Additional thanks go to Mark Troy of Texas A&M University for his assistance with technical administration of the survey and descriptive data analysis and to Kimberlee Pottberg of Texas A&M University for managing subcontracts and institutional contacts.

Finally, I would be remiss if I did not acknowledge the significant contributions of Jo Allen and James Anderson. Their encouragement and support allowed me to allocate time to the writing of this book and to formulate its chapters more clearly. After working together on undergraduate program review at North Carolina State University, we realized that our thoughts had truly come together. Not to acknowledge James and Jo would mean that I would have had to figure out where my thoughts ended and theirs began. This seemed impossible; thus, it is my privilege to include them in a special acknowledgment. In particular, I am grateful to Jo for editing the manuscript before it went to Stylus. Thank you, Jo!

Jo Allen is the Senior Vice President and Provost and Professor of English at Widener University. A tenured professor of English, she has just completed her two-year term as President of the Association of Teachers of Technical Writing, the largest academic organization of technical and professional communication scholars. She has published numerous books and articles and presented at national and international conferences on technical and professional communication and assessment. Prior to her move to Widener, Dr. Allen served as the Interim Vice Provost for Undergraduate Affairs at North Carolina State University and, previously, as a tenured faculty member and administrator at East Carolina University.

James Anderson is the Vice President for Student Success and Vice Provost for Institutional Assessment and Diversity at the State University of New York-Albany. This position takes a new approach to student affairs by building on student academic success and learning, strengthening the university's relationships with diverse people, and building community relations and outreach. From 2003 to 2005, Dr. Anderson served as Vice President and Associate Provost for Institutional Assessment and Diversity at Texas A&M University, and was a tenured professor in the department of psychology.

I

UNDERSTANDINGS OF
ASSESSMENT AND THE SCOPE
OF THIS BOOK

Perhaps one the most familiar mantras of teaching and learning is some version of a student's plea: "Don't tell me how to do something . . . show me."

This book attempts to do just that regarding assessment of student learning outcomes in the context of program review. Rather than telling readers how to conduct assessment, I have focused on institutions that are actively engaged in systematic evaluation of student learning and development, gathering meaningful data about how to improve student learning. I now seek to share the extent to which their efforts have been successful in transforming student learning and development, research, and service in a manner that is useful to others. This book seeks to share the good practices of institutions that have systematically made improvements in teaching/learning, research, and service, so that others may adapt the good practices to their own institutions. While the majority of the examples pertain to the teaching mission, these same practices can be adapted to service and research activities.

This book describes "good practices" in outcomes-based assessment program review in an effort to transform institutional decision making, particularly regarding student learning and development. Basic illustrative components of outcomes-based assessment program review are presented as are criteria for identifying good practices within outcomes-based assessment program review. Institutional case studies in outcomes-based assessment program review are woven throughout the book to illustrate principles of good practice. Finally, suggested steps for implementing sustainable outcomes-based assessment program review are outlined.

This book is intended for faculty and administrators responsible for implementing and sustaining outcomes-based assessment program review on their campuses. In addition, the book can help faculty and administrators understand the "what" and "why" of outcomes-based assessment program review. Furthermore, it explains the value of the outcomes-based assessment program review process.

Again, and important to note, this book is not a "how-to-do-assessment" book. There are several fine resources for that (see Bresciani, Zelna, & Anderson, 2004; Diamond, 1998; Huba & Freed, 2000; Lusthaus et al., 1999; Maki, 2004; Michelson, Mandel, et al., 2004; Nichols, 2002; Palomba & Banta, 1999; Stevens & Levi, 2004; Suskie, 2001, 2004; Tanner, 2001; Upcraft & Schuh, 1996; Wergin & Swigen, 2000). Rather, this book seeks to answer the questions: What does good outcomes-based assessment program review practice look like from an institutional perspective? Who is doing replicable work? In short, it couples fine assessment practices with cyclical program review so that the single process of outcomes-based assessment informs many purposes: program review, strategic planning, professional accreditation, institutional accreditation, and possibly even the assessment of general education.

Assessment and Accountability

This book is a timely contribution to the literature on outcomes-based assessment. Because legislatures and government agencies increasingly observe institutional practices and are involved in institutional decision making, accountability has become a prevalent concept and programmatic initiative (Allen and Bresciani, 2003; Ewell, 1997a; Ewell, 1997b; Ewell, 2003). To respond to growing demands for institutional accountability with regard to student learning and related expenditures, higher education requires an articulated definition of "quality education," rather than the ill-defined conceptualizations currently in use. For example, those engaged in quality-of-education conversations traditionally have used persistence and graduation rates as reliable indicators of such quality (Ewell, 1997a; Pike, 2001). These indicators are easy to define and measure, but do they identify the quality of the education students experience? Using these indicators, can one understand how well a student has learned the content and mechanics of his or her discipline or program? How well do faculty know whether a student has mastered problem solving or application of theory to practice? Indicators of persistence and graduation may indicate institutional type and mission, but they typically neglect more meaningful questions about the quality of learning outcomes.

Nationally standardized testing, whose ostensible purpose is to evaluate student learning across institutional types, is another traditional medium by which to measure the quality of education. Though standardized tests offer a relatively "simple" method of data collection, many tests are designed without consulting the curricula; thus, the tests do not measure the content of the course or program being delivered (Lopez, 1997; Maki & Bresciani, 2002). One solution is to require institutions to align their curricula with the content of the standardized test, a practice that typically reduces education to "teaching to the test." Additionally, such an approach neglects the particularities of institutional culture and its unique student populations to satisfy a standardized approach to higher education. Another consequence may be a decrease in the specialized information required for institutional and societal improvement. This trade-off may recreate the pattern of educating elites only, which practitioners have eschewed in favor of more equitable and accessible education (Anderson, Maki, & Bresciani, 2001). Yet another consequence may be that the information contained in the standardized tests may remain behind the learning curve of the research taking place in higher education, therefore widening the gap between postsecondary classroom learning and scholarly research. Additionally, standardized tests may be unable to accommodate varying learning styles (Anderson et al., 2001; Maki & Bresciani, 2002). Finally, the question is raised about whether using one standardized test to evaluate all students' learning is even responsible research. Which researchers do we know who engage in sound research methodology but use only one means of evaluation to formulate a theory or an assumption of quality?

Despite their claims of promoting quality and standards, legislators who call for strict quality monitoring actually appear to promote "watering down" educational principles because their proposals take simplistic approaches to evidence of learning. Moreover, the proposals often prevent the expression of faculty expertise and varying institutional values and resources (Bresciani, 2003). Some of these legislated indicators even distort conversations about quality. Institutions may feel compelled to seek traditional types of students and promote "cookie-cutter" institutional values in an effort to meet some standardized definition of a *quality institution* (Ewell, 2003). In reality, of course, different types of institutions are needed to serve different types of students with varying educational goals, such as an institution that educates adult single parents to become more effective managers, a research-intensive university where 60 percent of the student body leaves on a two-year religious mission, or a private liberal arts college whose students do not typically work more than twenty hours a week and who are most likely to obtain a bachelor's degree in four years (Bresciani, 2003). It is not difficult to see the obstacles in using any one test or set of indicators to assess the actual quality outcomes of the curriculum.

The challenge of finding meaningful quality indicators is exacerbated by a model of higher education that dates back to the mid- to late 1800s (Goodchild & Wechsler, 1989). Patterns and habits have become entrenched, and change in the delivery of higher education comes slowly, even when it is clearly needed. When government officials ask faculty and administrators to verify student outcomes, institutional responses are defensive, subversive, or nonexistent. Such avoidance behaviors manifest themselves because the inquiries and required indicators come from outside the academic discipline and institution (Bresciani, 2003). And, equally important, those stakeholders outside the academy—legislators, donors, parents, other educators, granting agencies, and so on—not only hold the purse strings for our endeavors, but they also control the barometer of public opinion, prestige, and general well-being for the academy. In short, refusing to answer these stakeholders' questions about academic quality is no longer an option and should not be an option.

Scrutiny of quality in higher education is not diminishing. In fact, educators face growing pressure to produce evidence of student learning, while faculty grow increasingly frustrated that their disciplinary expertise is under-appreciated or unrecognized (Bresciani, 2003). How, then, do institutions (1) report data on student learning and development in a meaningful way? (2) convey details about individual student learning so constituents can understand the quantity and quality of learning? and (3) inform decisions at a higher level while maintaining faculty research expertise and investment in teaching and learning?

An Overview of the Survey and Selected Participating Institutions

The criteria for this good practice study were founded on Seymour Papert's (1991) constructionist learning philosophy. "Papert's philosophy was used in the context that those delivering the learning are learning about how to improve student learning when they evaluate the delivery of their teaching, or those delivering the services are learning how to improve the services when they are evaluating the effectiveness of their services" (Bresciani, in press, p. 2). In this context, the concept of good practices emerges as those delivering the good practice engage in constructionist learning.

> It is in fact the teacher or the service provider who is constructing the best possible learning experience or service experience based on what they are learning about how well the entire package is working that constitutes opportunities for continuous improvement. This type of learning from doing and applying decisions to improve that which you are teaching in a manner that will align with the institutional culture within which you are working actually may appear to be more of a form of constructed relativism. (Bresciani, in press, p. 2)

For purposes of this book however, we base the study on a foundation of constructionist learning.

Therefore, good practice criteria were constructed and defined based on a set of criteria that emerged primarily from three key resources. The first is the *Nine Principles of Good Practice for Assessing Student Learning*, developed under the auspices of the American Association for Higher Education (AAHE) Assessment Forum, December 1992, found at http://www.buffalostate.edu/offices/assessment/aahe.htm. The second document is that of Eckel, Green, and Hill (2001), entitled *On Change V—Riding the Waves of Change: Insights from Transforming Institutions*, published by the American Council of Education. The third is criteria from Lopez's (2002) *Levels of Implementation* published by the Higher Learning Commission of the North Central, found at http://www.ncahigherlearningcommission.org/re sources/assessment/index.html.

Referring to these criteria, twenty-three of the most highly published assessment scholars in the United States were asked to identify institutions they felt met these criteria in the practice of their outcomes-based assessment program review. The research team made it clear that we were seeking institutions that had effective, efficient, and enduring practices and were interested in seeing good practice institutions at varying stages of their implementation. A list of forty-three institutions was generated and circulated to all of the assessment scholars for further comment. No institutions were removed from the list, and none was added.

All forty-three institutions were invited to participate in the study, which required participation in a survey of good practice that was designed as a part of a graduate research class using the criteria in the aforementioned references. We pilot-tested the survey in the class, and we used descriptive statistics to analyze the survey. In addition, we ran construct validity analysis, but the participant numbers in the survey were too low to establish any meaningful coefficients.

We also asked participants to submit a case study illustrating their good practice. Case study submissions ranged from seven to eighty-four pages in length. Using grounded theory (Strauss & Corbin, 1990), the primary author and graduate assistants reviewed the case studies to identify additional criteria not originally included in the survey.

This book comprises the summary of the good practice survey and the case study submissions. The research team modeled Papert's constructionist learning philosophy when compiling this work, as we allowed for each institution to refine the application of criteria to fit its needs, so the criteria and example practices in the book serve as guidelines. This is not a "one-size-fits-all, lockstep" application of good practice. It is intended to provide readers with ideas to consider for adapting to their own institutional culture.

Some good practice institutions elected not to participate in this study, and others may have been overlooked inadvertently because they have not yet become known for their exemplary assessment practices. Texas A&M University was included in the study because it is following implementation of this good practice model and, thus, is expected to emerge as a good practice institution. We are indebted to those institutions that took the time to submit their work so that all can benefit from the lessons they have learned.

In addition, while this book is intended to assist institutions in establishing institution-wide, outcomes-based assessment program review processes, the contents can be adapted to implementation of outcomes-based assessment program review in colleges, divisions, departments, or programs.

It bears repeating that this book is not intended to promote outcomes-based assessment program review as a process established merely to sustain itself. Rather, I intend to illustrate good practice in self-reflection that contributes to improved quality in student learning and development, teaching, research, and service. In other words, the process is not a means to its own end; rather, it is a way to engage systematically in daily critical inquiry about what works well and what needs to be improved (Maki, 2004).

2

WHY OUTCOMES-BASED UNDERGRADUATE ACADEMIC ASSESSMENT PROGRAM REVIEW IS SO IMPORTANT TO THE FUTURE OF HIGHER EDUCATION

Outcomes-based assessment is not a new term, nor is it new to higher education. Having at its core the inquiry-based notion of "how well do we know that what we are doing is working," assessment has been around in various versions for some time. In its earliest form and in regard to student learning, it dates back to 1063 CE at the University of Bologna, where outcomes-based assessment of student learning was known as juried reviews (Carroll, 2005). Here, the master teacher quizzed the student about what he[1] learned; in a window above the testing platform, another professor would stand, ensuring that the quality of the line of questioning was sound and that the student's responses were, in fact, acceptable for the level expected. This early form of inquiry was passed from academy to academy, and today we see its historical presence in university structures at the University of Bologna and at the Universidad de Salamanca, Spain, erected in 1230. This method of internal accountability for ensuring quality learning has continued in some form or another to the present day.

[1] The use of "he" is entirely appropriate here, indicating the practice of teaching only males at that time.

Internationally, quality assurance has had many faces. More recently, however, the quest to demonstrate quality in higher education and, in particular, quality in student learning, has been elevated to a global concern. In the European Union, countries prompted by the success of the Erasmus Mundus Programme (ERASMUS, http://europa.eu.int/comm/education/ programmes/mundus/index_en.html) have now moved on to other conversations around quality of higher education standards. ERASMUS was designed to encourage cooperation between the European Union (EU) and third-country institutions to improve accessibility and enhance the profile and visibility of higher education in the EU. While this effort has been beneficial, the European Higher Education Union—now comprising forty-five countries—has a more structured collaborative approach, complete with a quality assurance framework.

The Bologna Declaration of 1999 (http://www.bologna-berlin2003.de/ pdf/bologna_declaration.pdf) provides that collaborative framework and involves six principles. The Bologna Declaration consists of:

- a system of academic grades which are **easy to read and compare**, including the introduction of the diploma supplement (designed to improve international 'transparency' and facilitate academic and professional recognition of qualifications);
- a system essentially based on **two cycles**: a first cycle geared to the employment market and lasting at least three years and a second cycle (Master) conditional upon the completion of the first cycle;
- a system of **accumulation and transfer of credits** (of the ECTS [European Credit Transfer System] type already used successfully under Socrates-Erasmus);
- **mobility** of students, teachers and researchers;
- cooperation with regard to **quality assurance**;
- the **European dimension** of higher education. (from http://www .bologna-berlin2003.de/pdf/bologna_declaration.pdf)

The Bologna Declaration and its accompanying quality assurance framework, which was drafted in May 2005, provide the European Higher Education Union with the ability to demonstrate quality and transferability of that quality to create a powerful global educational force. Other countries, such as South Africa, Australia, and New Zealand, are also serious about their ability to identify quality in higher education. In addition, their central approaches to demonstrating quality in a transparent manner encourage their inclusion in global conversations about quality academic programs and over-all higher education experiences.

While the world continues its conversation about the quality of higher education within a framework called quality assurance, the United States has its own language for verifying the quality of student work. Since the United States has no central Ministry of Higher Education, the evolution of the conversation has not only used different language, it has taken a different course as well.

Peter Ewell (2002) illustrates the evolution of outcomes-based assessment in the United States in Banta and Associates' *Building a Scholarship of Assessment.* According to Ewell, early efforts to use information about how students learn to improve student learning dates back to the 1930s. The research at that time stemmed from a genuine desire to improve how students learn. As this effort expanded, it included research stemming from motivations to improve the underperforming student. Ewell further explains that over time, the outcomes-based assessment "movement" has had many influences, one of which has been business and industry.

Such movements as total quality management (TQM) (Dale & Bunney, 1999) and continuous quality improvement (CQI) (Frazier & Frazier, 1997) resembled the look and feel of outcomes-based assessment; however, the language with which they describe the processes used business terminology. While initiatives such as TQM and CQI are directly applicable to higher education, some faculty felt removed from the methodology because they did not recognize their own disciplinary link with these processes and the terminology used. Other faculty didn't understand the origin of these processes and decided, therefore, that they should be considered "fads" that would pass quickly and deserved no further consideration.

The reasons for growing faculty disconnect from evaluation of student learning and other business practices of higher education have a long history. This chapter does not discuss why faculty do not feel responsible for evaluating student learning, it just notes that it may be important to your faculty to understand, as was earlier illustrated, that evaluation of student learning that would inform improvements to instruction and the design of learning opportunities was a practice that was once inherent in the creation of student learning opportunities.

Because of the disconnect of faculty from the evaluation processes, efforts emerged to connect faculty and their interests more tightly to the inquiry approach of improving student learning and other administrative processes. As such, more authentic means of evaluation emerged, as did more emphasis on faculty involvement. It was posited that authentic assessment means and more direct faculty involvement could be embedded into traditionally established practices, such as institutional accreditation processes, and other evaluation and planning methods, such as TQM or program review (Palomba & Banta, 1999).

While institutions across the country were experiencing increasing success with these faculty-driven or faculty-dependent processes, the need for more pervasive practices and processes became readily evident. Pockets of successes were encouraging, yet authorities appeared to remain concerned about the overall state of affairs in U.S. higher education. How could we tell from these isolated practices that higher education was systematically improving across the nation?

Possibly, in response to concerns that faculty-driven assessment and authentic means would be undermined by an increasingly impatient desire to demonstrate quality of higher education in the United States, the Council of Regional Accrediting Commissions (CRAC) met to draft statements emphasizing the importance of placing student learning at the center of an institution and articulating good practices for evaluating that student learning. In 2003, all seven regional accrediting agencies in the United States agreed on principles of good practice that "would make the focus on student learning outcomes central to the accreditation process" (CRAC, p. 2). In addition, these agencies emphasized the importance of the involvement of faculty, co-curricular specialists, and all university stakeholders in the entire process for improving higher education and, in particular, for improving student learning.

In 2004, CRAC drafted another document to serve as a guide for all institutions desiring to become more learning centered. This booklet is filled with advice that can assist an institution in its self-reflection process. While the principles and recommended criteria it includes pertain to the evaluation of student learning, the same principles can be applied to the evaluation of all the services within an institution that support student learning. If you think about it in this context, while this is a book on good practices in program review and includes principles that can apply to student services as well as other administrative services, first answering the standard question, "how does this program contribute to student learning in this institution?" is an important place to start in the self-reflection process. The booklet is filled with additional questions that an institution can ask itself. The questions posed support the good practice findings of this study.

It is evident from this discussion that outcomes-based assessment and its pervasive practice are necessary to the improvement of higher education; however, it is not evident how an institution can meaningfully engage in those practices. Thus, the purpose of this book comes into play. Its intent, as noted in the first chapter, is to provide those who desire to engage meaningfully in an organic process with some ideas and examples of how to do so. Thus far, no time frame has been established for higher education having to prove that good practices of assessment, such as those presented in the following pages, have resulted in better higher education in the United States or improved student learning. However, the many conversations stirring at the time of publication of this book may soon change that.

At the time of this writing, some of those in authority may be influenced by the *No Child Left Behind Act* (http://www.ed.gov/nclb/landing.jhtml?src-=pb) and may require regional accreditors or states to use standardized tests or other performance indicators, such as those included in *Measuring Up* (http://measuringup.highereducation.org/2002/reporthome.htm) or *U.S. News and World Report* (http://www.usnews.com/usnews/edu/grad/rankings/edu/eduindex_brief.php), to demonstrate the level of quality in higher education. However, as we have discussed in chapter 1, such broad indicators do not fully indicate the level of quality in student learning, nor do they tend to lead to meaningful and purposeful decisions for improvement or maintain access to higher education. Therefore, while standardized tests may add value for comparative discussions, the value of reflecting faculty's expertise and the benefits of social justice may be lost if genuine outcomes-based assessment is not used.

Conversations within the International Network for Quality Assurance Agencies in Higher Education (INQAAHE), established in 1991, support the academic autonomy of faculty and universities. The INQAAHE is an organization whose members consist of individual countries' quality assurance and accreditation agencies. Its draft policy statement, under the heading "Primacy of Academic Freedom and Integrity," declares:

> While higher education comes in many forms, the Network holds that the defining characteristics of higher education include clear policy and procedural commitments to academic integrity and academic freedom, which is the recognition that academic endeavors should be wholly conducted in a

spirit of honesty and openness. External quality assurance should be conducted in such a way as to promote academic freedom and intellectual and institutional integrity. [http://www.inqaahe.org/docs/Policy%20State ment%20(Draft%203).doc]

This statement promotes and reinforces practices that allow for faculty and co-curricular expertise to be respected and for unique institutional cultures to be valued, while institutions pursue quality and integrity in their offerings and practices. In summary, INQAAHE supports and promotes good practices in genuine outcomes-based assessment.

While business and industry have an impact on quality conversation in higher education in the United States, it is unclear how the international trade agreements (http://www.tradeineducation.org/general_info/frames-.html) will affect these conversations about quality. Other countries are taking note and anticipating that these agreements will provide them with further opportunities to demonstrate the quality of higher learning they currently deliver.

Finally, with the Homeland Security Act (http://www.whitehouse.gov/-deptofhomeland/analysis/) potentially correlating with a loss of 38 percent in international undergraduate student enrollment in the United States in fall 2004 (NAFSA, 2004), the future of this and other such acts may assist other countries in advancing their educational agendas.

Regardless of what legislation may come, the following chapters provide an overview of how genuine outcomes-based assessment program review may assist the United States in its efforts to systematically improve and demonstrate the current quality of higher education in the United States, if not for comparative accountability purposes then for the general desire to improve the quality of education and to improve the underperforming student.

3

OVERVIEW OF OUTCOMES-BASED ASSESSMENT PROGRAM REVIEW

While "outcomes-based assessment" may seem to be a catch-phrase, the previous chapters illustrate that the intention behind outcomes-based assessment—that of quality assurance and external accountability in higher education—has been around for a while. Today, there are many definitions for outcomes-based assessment.

Maki (2004) posits that outcomes-based assessment is a systematic means to satisfy educators' innate intellectual curiosity about how well their students learn what educators say they are learning. Suskie (2004) writes that assessment is writing clear, measurable outcomes; ensuring students have opportunities to reach those outcomes; implementing a systematic evaluation system; and then using the results to improve student learning. Hernon and Dugan (2004) define assessment as "the process of gathering and assembling data in an understandable form" (p. 8). There are several other definitions of assessment and outcomes-based assessment, some varying a great deal from one another, as they are embedded in various academic disciplines (e.g., psychology, medicine, etc.).

When implementing outcomes-based assessment at an institution, it is extremely important to have a group of faculty and practitioners come together to define outcomes-based assessment so that it has meaning to those who implement it (Bresciani, Zelna, & Anderson, 2004). Some institutions, such as Sinclair Community College, chose to borrow a definition from the literature, while others, such as Alverno College, developed one from conversations with faculty and staff. See appendix B for sample definitions of outcomes-based assessment from good practice institutions.

While each of these good practice institutions has adopted its own definition of assessment, for this book I offer the following working definition for outcomes-based assessment program review:

> Outcomes-based assessment program review is a systematic process in which program faculty and/or professionals articulate the intended results of the cumulative contribution of their program. In outcomes-based assessment, faculty and co-curricular professionals articulate what the program intends to accomplish in regard to its services, research, student learning, and faculty/staff development programs. The faculty and/or professionals then purposefully plan the program so that the intended results (i.e., outcomes) can be achieved; implement methods to systematically—over time—identify whether the end results *have* been achieved; and, finally, use the results to plan improvements or make recommendations for policy consideration, recruitment, retention, resource reallocation, or new resource requests. This systematic process of evaluation is then repeated at a later date to determine whether the program improvements contribute to the intended outcomes.

Keep in mind that while an institution may have one definition for outcomes-based assessment program review, practitioners may need to be flexible in interpreting the definition so it can accommodate the needs of individual professional accreditation units and/or professional standards. For some, the institutional definition may provide all the flexibility that is needed. For example, at North Carolina State University, the definition of outcomes-based assessment program review took into account the most rigorous professional program accreditation requirements and standards operating in the programs at the university, so that it could meet all of the other professional accreditation requirements in effect at the university. If this is not the case at your institution, you may need to create crosswalks (e.g., ways of illustrating that the word used by a professional accrediting agency, such as objective, may have the same meaning as a different word used by the institution, such as outcome) from individual college and division definitions to the university definition.

Most important, the definition of outcomes-based assessment program review should reinforce that it is not a process designed to be merely self-propagating and self-contained—it exists to provide educators, researchers, and practitioners with information to satisfy their own natural curiosity about the results of their work. The information gleaned from the process informs conversations about accountability and opportunities for improvement. To reiterate, the process is not a means unto its own end; it is a way to engage systematically in critical daily inquiry about discovering what works well and what needs to be improved (Maki, 2004).

An example of an institution whose definition embodies the purpose of the process, rather than a process built to sustain itself, is Miami University of Ohio. Its definition of assessment states,

> An effective assessment answers the question, "How well are our students meeting the four Miami Plan goals of critical thinking, understanding contexts, engaging with other learners, and reflecting and acting?" The assessment must provide authentic information to the department to (1) improve student learning and development in the four Miami Plan goal areas, and (2) make changes in courses to continuously improve students' learning and development. (Submitted by Jerry Stillwater, Miami University of Ohio)

At Oregon State University, members of the student affairs assessment council realized after completing an internal audit that they needed to engage in conversation about what assessment means. The assessment council's "initial learning agenda was designed to respond to these questions: (1) What do we need to know to be able to help departments become more aligned around departmental and program assessment and review? (2) What sort of structure is needed to support departmental efforts? (3) How do we set up a context and reporting structure that will institutionalize a systematic review of programs in student affairs?"

The council decided that it was important to have a shared understanding of the following:

- Purpose of assessment and program review
- Terminology and definitions
- The practical and theoretical context

- The difference between collecting data and actually developing a plan with questions about programs, services, student learning
- How others had done what they were trying to do
- Practices already in place that could be built on
- A format and system of reporting plans for review, results, decisions, and so on that respected the different disciplines or services represented in the division
- How the work could be sustained (submitted by Rebecca Sanderson and Larry Roper, Oregon State University; more information on Oregon State University's process can be found at http://styluspub.com/resources/outcomes-basedprogramreview.aspx).

Political Motivation for Outcomes-Based Assessment

It is important to recognize the reason your institution wants to become involved in outcomes-based assessment program review. In some cases, the political environment of an institution may make it difficult to implement the good practices of assessment presented in this book. For example, if the leadership of an institution is mandating outcomes-based assessment solely as a means of appeasing the university's accreditation requirements, it may be difficult to implement a genuine practice of self-reflection. (Note that it is becoming increasingly difficult to appease an accreditor by "faking" your institutional commitment to assessment.) Furthermore, engaging in outcomes-based assessment program review for the primary purpose of defending a program is troublesome because the defensive posture obscures the true purpose of assessment. Furthermore, if an institution focuses only on evidence to bolster the program, valuable discoveries about the program may be overlooked.

It should become clearer as you read on why it has become increasingly difficult for institutions to be disingenuous about outcomes-based assessment program review processes as they go through their regional accreditation process. To avoid the perception of disingenuous self-evaluation, it may be beneficial simply to acknowledge the key role accreditation requirements play in assessment initiatives while you are making the process your own, as California State University, Sacramento (CSUS), does:

Assessment at CSUS is a University-wide unit based process to determine how well and in what ways individual units and the University are meeting their individual and collective goals. It was established by the Administration and the Academic Senate in response to a directive and guidelines from WASC. Assessment is an ongoing process, required of all units in the University and conducted by the members of each unit. Assessment will become part of the program review process (this includes both Academic Program Review and Student Services Review), and as part of the program review process it will tie into the planning of the unit. The primary goal of assessment is to improve the educational program at CSUS (http://www .csus.edu/acaf/Assessment/why.stm, 2004; more information on CSUS's process can be found at http://styluspub.com/resources/outcomes-based programreview.aspx).

Implementers at Hampden-Sydney recognize that "the final level of their review occurs in the college's decennial reaffirmation of accreditation by the Southern Association of Colleges and Schools (SACS). In this review we must demonstrate that we assess the educational outcomes of our programs. For at least two cycles of SACS's reaffirmation of accreditation we have received acknowledgment of the extent, depth, and seriousness of the outcomes assessment of our Rhetoric Program" (submitted by Elizabeth J. Deis and Earl Fleck, Hampden-Sydney College; more information on Hampden-Sydney College's process can be found at http://styluspub.com/ resources/outcomes-basedprogramreview.aspx). Even in this example, one can see the delicate balance between the accrediting agency's expectations and the university's adaptation to make the required process meaningful and manageable. Rather than pretending this requirement does not exist, they choose to implement procedures that bring the requirement to life and demonstrate its value to the faculty and staff engaged in implementing outcomes-based assessment.

Balancing the perceived "stick" of accreditors and the "carrot" of the value gained from doing the work well, where results actually inform decisions for improvement, may sometimes feel overwhelming. However, if the "stick" and "carrot" are not in balance, political motivations for engaging in the process may derail outcomes-based assessment as easily as overzealous practitioners who just think that "everyone should just get it (for example, outcomes-based assessment) and do it." While we discuss in detail in later chapters strategies for keeping these two motivations in balance, this is an opportunity to emphasize the importance of faculty and staff committees, which rotate and provide the implementers with renewed voices and fresh perspectives and concerns. These perspectives are invaluable to maintain the balance of the carrot and the stick, while also promoting learning and practice about assessment throughout a larger group of faculty and practitioners.

Isothermal Community College models this balance well through committee work. In 1998 Isothermal established a volunteer assessment task force that was added to an already established umbrella structure, called TALC— the Team for the Advancement of a Learning College. The composition of the original task force was evenly mixed between administrators and faculty; now the task force is 80 percent faculty and 20 percent administration. The continuous cycling of faculty and administrators with an increasing representation of faculty has kept the committee's perspectives fresh and in touch with those who implement outcomes-based assessment program review every day. (More information on Isothermal's process can be found at http://styluspub.com/resources/outcomes-basedprogramreview.aspx.)

Conceptual Framework and Common Operational Language

While deciding on an institutional definition of assessment is an important first step, an equally important endeavor is to articulate the institution's conceptual framework or philosophy for assessment and, thus, a common language to use when implementing the process (Bresciani et al., 2004). Many institutions struggle with implementing outcomes-based assessment program review simply because faculty and practitioners do not understand the purpose, goals, or intended outcomes of the activity or why they are being asked to participate. Finally, faculty and staff often become frustrated by not understanding the language of outcomes-based assessment. For example, what one person refers to as an *objective*, another might call a goal or a means to accomplish an outcome.

Gathering faculty and administrators together to draft the underlying philosophy for your institution's engagement in outcomes-based program review will help faculty and staff to explore the value of the work and apply it within the culture of their own institution or unit. In the conceptual framework or philosophy of practice document, faculty and staff can learn to better understand the purpose of rigorous self-reflection. The "what is in it for me" question can be addressed and answered in language that can be understood across disciplines. The political nature of outcomes-based assessment begins to dissolve as faculty and staff themselves articulate the benefits of formalizing what innately occurs in their day-to-day work (Bresciani et al., 2004; Maki, 2004).

Furthermore, the conceptual framework provides an opportunity to emphasize the learning-centered nature of the institution. It is within the conceptual framework that values for improvement and the motivation for that improvement come to life. Here, institutions can demonstrate whether they recognize the connection of inquiry within research to inquiry in learning and service. The commitment to improve all facets of the university does not have to isolate them from one another, and that can be made clear in the conceptual framework document.

When constructing a conceptual framework or guiding principles for outcomes-based program review and a common operational language, a few guidelines may prove beneficial:

1. Engage in these conversations faculty and staff who are well respected in their disciplines and in their research. This helps alleviate the common misperception that outcomes-based assessment is just another fad or a process built by administrators to "check up" on the work of faculty. Also, seeing their own colleagues—rather than just "assessment cheerleaders"—involved in drafting foundational documents can help to overcome the concerns of those who question the meaning and motivation behind the process. They may also be more likely to read the document itself and find meaning in it.

2. Incorporate the definition of "outcomes-based assessment" into the conceptual framework. A disconnect between the language used in the definition and that used in the conceptual framework is confusing, and faculty and staff may think that two distinct processes are being implemented.

3. Allow the conceptual framework to guide the use of a common operational language for outcomes-based assessment program review. Having the same language in the program review guidelines as in the conceptual framework, for example, makes the process even more meaningful to the faculty and staff who will implement it. This practice also reduces the confusion about more than one process being implemented.

4. Allow faculty and staff to use language and literature citations that are appropriate for their discipline. Also, encourage emphasis of the unique institutional culture in all of the basic documentation. This emphasis makes the process more meaningful to faculty and staff while celebrating the institution's unique culture. While you may prefer certain definitions and certain assessment scholars, allow the faculty to explore others and to incorporate literature from their own disciplines. In appendix C are various conceptual frameworks and philosophies for outcomes-based assessment program review. Each uses different language and literature references. Note, for example, how an institution such as Alverno College uses the term "scholarship of teaching and learning," while others use the term "the science of learning."

5. Provide meaningful opportunities to share the conceptual framework in such a manner that other faculty and staff (who may not have contributed to writing it) have the opportunity to comment on the documents and offer suggestions. Such discourse raises awareness about the purposes of engaging in outcomes-based assessment and can lead to more effective ways of communicating these purposes. Furthermore, while you may reach consensus on the foundational documents, faculty and staff may want to recast the conceptual framework somewhat differently for individual departments so that more faculty and staff can identify with the language and the process. Crosswalks of language can always be written to illustrate the commonalities and aid communication. It is important to allow this type of flexibility as it enhances meaning and engagement. Later on, it will be important to revisit all these frameworks to ensure that one shared institutional conceptual understanding still remains.

6. Use the conceptual definition, framework/philosophy, and common language documents to implement outcomes-based assessment program review so everyone is continually reminded of the positive result of his or her work, rather than of some aspect of the process. Many of these good practice institutions have been implementing and refining their process anywhere from five to thirty years. Over the years, conversations about what it means to become engaged in outcomes-based assessment arise continually, and faculty and staff often become mired in details that can detract from the ultimate goal of outcomes-based

assessment program review. Maintaining and reminding people of the overarching purpose of outcomes-based assessment program review may reduce the amount of time faculty and staff spend on details that may not be that important.

When constructing the conceptual framework or philosophy-of-assessment document, it also may be helpful to incorporate some of the work developed by the model for program assessment researched in the Pew report on learning-centered institutions (Doherty, Riordan, & Roth, 2002). Here, the researchers posit that program, curriculum, and institution-wide assessment should be implemented so the institution becomes a learning-centered organization. They suggest that a learning-centered institution

- is integral to learning about student learning,
- creates processes that assist faculty, staff, and administrators to improve student learning,
- involves inquiry to judge program value and effectiveness for fostering student learning,
- generates multiple sources of feedback to faculty, staff, and administrators about patterns of student and alumni performance in relation to learning outcomes that are linked to the curriculum,
- makes comparisons of student and alumni performance to standards, criteria, or indicators (faculty, disciplinary, professional, accrediting, certifying, legislative) to create public dialogue,
- yields evidence-based judgments of how students and alumni benefit from the curriculum, co-curriculum, and other learning contexts, and
- guides curricular, co-curricular, institution-wide improvements. (pp. 3–14)

Encouraging faculty and staff to articulate what outcomes-based assessment program review means to them furthers the goal of creating a process of self-reflection for "thinking people" (T. Benberg, personal communication, December 7, 2003). It stimulates faculty and staff's own innate intellectual curiosity and inquiry (Maki, 2004), and it helps clarify the value of self-reflection, thus encouraging faculty and staff to make time for their intentional practice (Rodrigues, 2002; Wergin, 1999). Participants at Isothermal Community College testify that the inspiration they gained from the Alverno College model for faculty inclusion kept their faculty talking about assessment, resulting in the development of their criteria and rubrics, but also advancing the emergence of faculty teamwork and leadership for their out-comes-based assessment program review process.

The common operational language document may be incorporated fully into the conceptual framework document, such as at Sinclair Community College; it may be a completely separate document, such as Texas A&M University's; or it may be a separate document and be included in a fre-quently asked questions (FAQ) document, such as North Carolina State University's. Regardless of how the document is organized, the point is that these institutions' faculty and staff understand what each word used in out-comes-based assessment program review means. For example, what is the difference between an objective and an outcome? Many disciplines, as well as professional accrediting agencies, may define those terms differently. Thus, having an institutional definition for those terms will assist in the abil-ity of faculty to communicate across disciplines. This understanding helps faculty and staff talk across programs and discuss the shared learning or chal-lenges that may be occurring and that they are identifying through their as-sessment practices. Appendix D has some examples of common language documents.

In some cases, it may be wise to provide links if the institutional com-mon language you use is different from one of the program's professional accrediting agencies'. For example, if you have an ABET-accredited program and you are using "objectives" as goals in your institutional common lan-guage, you may want to provide a link to what "objectives" means to ABET reviewers. This helps avoid confusion.

In some institutions, because of their historical context for developing outcomes-based assessment program review, divisions have been split in their implementation. Given the institutional history, and provided that some ad-ministrators desire not to proceed with changing language that has already been embedded into the organizational culture, it also may be a matter of building an institutional link. For example, at one Maryland community col-lege, program review has been implemented and developed in two separate areas, student affairs and academic affairs. As all of the community colleges came together to adopt a common language for working on shared institu-tional learning principles, they found themselves dealing with yet another common language. Building a link such as the one below helped their faculty and staff to avoid confusion and frustration.

Student Affairs Word	Academic Affairs Word	MD Community College Word
Vision	= Purpose	= Mission
Objective	= Goals	= Goals
Outcomes	= Objectives	= Outcomes

The Program Review Guidelines

Effective outcomes-based academic and co-curricular program review processes are designed to be intentionally reflective and purposefully planned. While this book provides the readers with some templates for consideration, the most important concept to remember is that the design of the self-evaluation process must have meaning to the faculty and the administrators who implement it. Therefore, throughout the good practice cases, you will see deviations from the suggested template so that you can determine for your institution the most meaningful way to engage in purposeful self-reflection.

Before sharing template designs, keep in mind that we are emphasizing outcomes-based assessment program review. In an effort to make program review more meaningful, many institutions, such as Indiana University–Purdue University Indianapolis (IUPUI) and Truman State University, incorporated the outcomes assessment process early on in their program review process. Doing so enhanced the utility of the review process's findings. The institutions listed in this book have also incorporated outcomes-based assessment into their program review processes and, thus, into their program review guidelines. (More information on IUPUI's process can be found at http://styluspub.com/resources/outcomes-basedprogramreview.aspx.)

Each of the good practice institutions listed in this book (a detailed listing is included in the acknowledgment section and in appendix A) has a different set of program review guidelines. Some of those guidelines can be found in appendix E. You can see the variance in each set of guidelines, yet they share some similarities, which are discussed in detail in chapter 4.

What is most important to keep in mind when constructing guidelines is not to request information that may not be meaningful to a program's self-evaluation process. If your intent is *not* to assign "busy" work, then be careful what you ask programs to complete as a part of your program review process. North Carolina State University uses "commonsense" criteria when reviewing its guidelines. It simply asks:

- Why do we want programs to submit this information?
- How will this piece of information help the program discern whether they are meeting their program goals or institutional goals, if applicable?
- How will this piece of information help us to understand the program's current quality and aspiration for quality? (Submitted by North Carolina State's Committee on Undergraduate Program Review)

It may be wise to keep institutional program guidelines at a minimum and maintain flexibility within the program review guideline requirements, so that if some disciplines or administrative programs want to add sections of their program review to accommodate professional accreditation processes and administrative standards, they can do so without having to explain in detail to other administrative units why they have included the additional sections.

Regardless of which route you choose, keep in mind that if programs have already gone through a descriptive process—a process where they have already reported to the institution what they do and who is involved—this might be the time to incorporate outcomes-based assessment so the inquiry of what works well can be embedded into the self-reflection and provide additional meaning to the descriptive process already completed.

Some good practice institutions have very specific guidelines for their outcomes-based assessment program review processes. At California State University, Sacramento, the guidelines require program self-studies to include three levels of assessment: (1) a statement of mission, goals, and learning objectives; (2) two indirect and one direct measure of the learning objectives; and (3) reflection, discussion, and conclusions based on assessment results. (For an explanation of "indirect" and "direct" methods of assessment, see the template element, entitled "Evaluation Methods for Each Outcome," in the following section. (The guidelines for their self-study can be found at http://www.csus.edu/acaf/univmanual/acaprgmrev.htm#SS.)

At California State University, Monterey Bay, the guidelines follow a specific template as well, and then pose a series of questions to consider when reporting the learning outcomes. An example excerpted from http://policy.csumb.edu/policies/approved_policies/program_review_model/ follows.

Guiding review questions for self-study:

1. Program Mission and Goals
2. Major Learning Outcomes (MLOs)

- Do the MLOs describe learning outcomes in terms of observable and assessable student behaviors?
- Are the MLOs clear, concise, and unambiguous?
- Do the MLOs describe complex, higher-order knowledge and skills?
- To what extent does the set of MLOs represent a scope and depth of student learning which are appropriate for a baccalaureate degree?
- To what extent will achievement of the MLOs prepare students for the societal service, employment, and graduate school opportunities articulated by the program?

3. Assessment Protocol for Each MLO
   - How clearly does the assessment protocol stipulate the types of documentation students should or may submit as evidence of learning for each MLO?
   - How clearly does the protocol identify the criteria that will be used to review student work or documentation for each MLO?
   - How clearly does the assessment protocol explain the standards that will be used to rate student work?
   - Overall, to what extent does the protocol represent a valid assessment of student learning related to the MLOs?
   - Does the protocol emphasize consistency between assessors and between assessment venues?

4. Student Learning
   - To what extent are students developing the expected knowledge and skills in the program?
   - To what extent does the program collect and maintain summative evidence of student learning in the program?
   - To what extent does the program collect the type of information to enable it to gauge student growth during the program?
   - Does the program have a plan for using evidence of student learning as a means of assessing its program effectiveness and improvement?

Alverno College, on the other hand, has no stated program review guidelines. Its intent is to encourage faculty members to be thoughtful and purposeful in selecting what they review. The Alverno guidelines are as follows:

Taking a departmental and institutional perspective can call for a variety of approaches, strategies, and processes. These include:

- review of current theory, scholarship, and practice;
- clarifying learning outcomes, abilities, and criteria—and developing ways to assess them at the program or institutional level;

- evaluation of general education and the major field;
- longitudinal analysis of changes in student and alumnae abilities, learning, and development as a result of curriculum and college culture, who changes, who benefits and why; studying students' and alumnae perspectives on learning and causal attributions to curriculum and college culture; studying graduates' career advancement;
- studying the performance of alumnae abilities in work, personal, and civic roles; and of outstanding professionals who are not Alverno graduates;
- practitioner-based inquiry studies;
- validating the ability-based performance assessment process (student assessment-as-learning);
- making a case for the value, worth, and effectiveness of the college and curriculum. (2004, http://depts.alverno.edu/ere/ipa/ipa.html)

In the Alverno College guidelines, you saw three different means of requesting outcomes-based assessment program review portfolios. Most of those reasons for the differences in the formats have to do with the institutional culture within which program review is carried out. This is a very important point. In each case, these are not the program review guideline templates that existed when these universities first engaged in outcomes-based assessment program review. Each institution's process has evolved as its culture surrounding outcomes-based assessment has evolved. In Alverno's case, after more than thirty years of perfecting this process and embedding it into the day-to-day doings of faculty, staff, and students, very little guidance is needed when asking for the program review report. The habits of purposeful self-reflection are so ingrained, there is little need for written guidelines for describing documented evidence.

To provide readers with some suggestions of what would make their program review process an outcomes-based assessment program review process, I provide an outcomes-based assessment plan template based on the good practice literature review mentioned earlier, the good practice survey, and the good practice case studies. Again, remember that this template is just that, a template. Your institution's faculty and administrators need to determine how best to create or refine your institution's own template to make the process meaningful and manageable at your own institution. Examples of good practice applications of this template can be found in appendix F.

In addition, keep in mind that each institution may infer different meanings for these particular elements of the template. For purposes of this study, I provided a brief description of each element to the good practice institution. Detailed descriptions of each element from various institutions can be found in the common operational language examples in appendix D.

Template Elements for Outcomes-Based Assessment Program Review

Program Name and Description

As ridiculous as it may sound, I have seen institutions struggle with meaningful outcomes-based assessment because there was no general description of the program being evaluated. In other words, it was difficult to interpret evidence for continuous improvement if the program could not be identified or generally understood. Including the program name and description also helps to clarify which programs incorporate which degrees or services into their self-evaluation. For example, some service or programming departments may want to subdivide their programs by thematic ways of delivering the programs, such as leadership development and programming for the general student body. In other cases, administrative units that have to evaluate both programming and facilities use, such as student unions and residence halls, might find it useful to divide their program review processes to accommodate such varying roles and missions. However, some departments may want to incorporate all of these types of responsibilities into one program review as one facet of the program and its outcomes is dependent upon the other. For example, a program may not be able to illustrate fully while its educational learning outcomes are hindered if it doesn't refer to limitations discovered in the facilities (i.e., classrooms, etc.) where learning occurs.

Some academic programs may choose to have a program review document for each of their degree programs; others may want to have one for their entire department. Again, there is no one "right" way. The program or department should engage in outcomes-based assessment program review in a manner that makes the most sense to it. Therefore, one department may have three degree programs, but since they all share some general learning outcomes, they may choose to have only one program review document;

another department may have as many program review documents as it has specializations.

One hundred percent of the institutions in this study require programs to submit their names and a brief description of the program. Eighty-seven percent of them also reported that use of the program names and descriptions is somewhat to very important in making decisions for continuous improvement.

Program Mission Statement

Similar to the aforementioned reason for providing a brief description of the program, 87 percent of the institutions in this study require each program to include a brief statement articulating the purpose of the program. And that same percentage reported that the mission statement was somewhat to very important in making decisions about continuous improvement.

Many institutional accreditors, such as the New England Association of Schools and Colleges (NEASC) and the Middle States Commission on Higher Education (MSCHE), and professional accreditors such as the National Architectural Accrediting Board (NAAB) encourage programs to articulate mission statements not only so that program faculty and administrators can determine how well their individual programs align with institutional and division mission statements, but also so that program faculty can determine how well the program's mission statement relates to the regional accreditor perspective, as in the case of NAAB. In regard to the Southern Association of Colleges and Schools (SACS), the ability to demonstrate that a "coherent course of study is compatible with its stated purpose" (SACS, 2002) is also important.

In addition to addressing accreditation requirements, another reason for articulating a mission statement is that, for many programs, it is the first step in the process of being able to articulate end results of the doing. If an organization can articulate a general and brief description of what the program is about, that description may help it articulate general goals and, later, more specific outcomes (Bresciani et al., 2004).

Program Goals

Ninety-three percent of the institutions in this good practice study require each program to submit statements that generally describe what the program intends to accomplish or deliver. For example, program goals could be written for enrollment, research, faculty development, service, or academic or co-curricular initiatives. Ninety-three percent also reported that program goals were somewhat to very important in making decisions for continuous improvement.

Program goals help program faculty and administrators focus on delivery of the program. This may aid in both planning and assessment as program faculty and administrators can identify how they intend to achieve their program mission through various steps and methods.

Program goals can also capture the vision and/or value statements that inspire us to do what we want to accomplish (Bresciani et al., 2004). Broad statements such as "students will be exposed to opportunities to appreciate the arts and literature" or "students will value diversity," embody what we want to have happen as a result of the learning in the program; thus, we need to make sure students have had opportunities to learn about art and literature and how society benefits from art and literature. We cannot necessarily identify "appreciation" or "value," yet this is not the level where we need to be able to distinguish that type of detail.

Likewise, goals help researchers make statements such as "to provide cutting-edge discoveries in the area of blood cell tissue regeneration." Such a goal helps the program planner and the faculty research team design a lab that will be conducive to this kind of discovery. But to determine whether discoveries have actually been made or whether the lab is properly equipped and staffed, the faculty team needs to articulate outcomes to identify whether the goals have been met and to implement the means to evaluate these outcomes. In this example, some of the outcomes will most likely be derived from their research hypothesis. To illustrate this process, consider an example from a good practice institution.

Each year, the Hampden-Sydney College Rhetoric Program establishes an outcomes assessment project. The staff works from the program's goals and objectives, selecting one or more of the objectives as the focus for the year's assessment project. Sometimes the faculty's engagement in a project leads them to examine related issues, thus extending the assessment work beyond a single year. However, these assessment projects always begin with an examination of their list of goals and objectives, with a keen awareness of how their goals relate to the overall educational goals and the Quality Enhancement Plan of Hampden-Sydney College (submitted by Elizabeth J. Deis and Earl Fleck).

Program Outcomes

Outcomes statements are the point at which the mission and goals come to life. One hundred percent of the institutions in this study require each program to include statements that specifically describe the result of the program activities for enrollment, research, faculty development, service, academic, or co-curricular initiatives. That same proportion reported that program outcomes are somewhat to very important in making decisions for continuous improvement.

The SACS regional accreditor requires that "the institution identifies expected outcomes for its educational programs and its administrative and educational support services; assesses whether it achieves these outcomes; and provides evidence of improvement based on analysis of those results" (SACS, 2004). Similar statements can be found in WASC, North Central Association Commission on Accreditation and School Improvement (NCA), MSCHE, and NEASC materials.

Program outcomes and learning outcomes, which follow, are the heart and soul of outcomes-based assessment program review. Rather than program reviews existing purely as a descriptive review process, they allow program faculty and administrators to reflect on what they intend to accomplish and organize and plan activities and resources to better achieve those end results, thus demonstrating more accountability for what they are trying to accomplish and the extent to which it is being accomplished through articulating outcomes, gathering and reporting results, and making decisions or recommendations.

Student Learning Outcomes

All but one of the institutions included in this study require each program to write curricular or co-curricular student learning outcomes that depict cognitive abilities and affective dimensions that the program wants to instill or enhance in students, faculty, and staff (the one exception does not require drafting of co-curricular learning outcomes). These statements typically describe results of teaching or out-of-class experiences that facilitate learning. They also include outcomes for staff and faculty development programs. All of the institutions that require student learning outcomes reported that such outcomes are somewhat to very important in making decisions for continuous improvement.

Similar to the statement on program outcomes, those same regional accrediting agencies have strong statements about how each program should specify learning outcomes in the curricular and co-curricular programs. While some professional accreditors have yet to strongly request articulation of student learning outcomes, many have. Professional accreditors such as the Accreditation Board for Engineering and Technology (ABET) and the National Council for Accreditation of Teacher Education (NCATE) clearly articulate the need for such definitive outcomes. While the Association to Advance Collegiate Schools of Business (AACSB) does not use the outcomes language, it does express its intent for programs to focus on learning via goals.

In primarily administrative programs that do not have accreditation standards, organizations that promote standards are also moving to outcomes language. The Council for the Advancement of Standards in Higher Education (CAS) provides program and student learning outcomes examples in its most recent 2003 publication, which provides guidelines and standards and aids administrative units in evaluating results of their activities.

Assessment of student learning outcomes is at the heart of program review at IUPUI:

> Each review team is charged specifically with the responsibility of considering and commenting on the impact of the unit's programs on student learning. Nevertheless, the review process is comprehensive. Thus student learning is viewed in the context of faculty credentials and areas of expertise, curriculum structures, instructional strategies, scholarship and research activities, and evidence of civic engagement. Both undergraduate and graduate programs, where they exist, are considered in a single review; and students, faculty, staff, and administration are all under scrutiny. (Submitted by Trudy Banta and Karen Black, IUPUI)

This approach exemplifies the learning-centered institution, and regardless of its institutional mission and type, this approach demonstrates that learning and the improvement of learning is valued.

Evaluation Methods for Each Outcome

To evaluate program and/or learning outcomes, a program has to understand how best to approach the methodology for each particular assessment challenge. Eighty percent of the institutions in this study require each program to describe the methods used to evaluate specific outcomes, and 73 percent require that the programs detail the criteria that will illustrate within the evaluation method how the faculty and administrators know that the outcomes have been reached. The same percentages respectively report the somewhat to very important use of the methods and criteria in making decisions for continuous improvement.

While the regional accreditors do not specify which evaluation methods programs must use, many intend to identify whether the programs have used multiple methods of evaluation. Furthermore, some professional accreditors, such as ABET and AACSB, even specify that a program must use direct and indirect measures of evaluation. While such evaluation methods are often left to the program to define, ABET, for example, states that indirect measures such as "[s]tudent self-assessment, opinion surveys, and course grades are not, by themselves or collectively, acceptable methods for documenting the achievement of outcomes" (2004, p. 2).

Palomba and Banta (1999) define direct evidence as methods of collecting information that require the students to demonstrate their knowledge and skills and indirect evidence as those that ask students or someone else to reflect on student learning. Using Peter Ewell's (2003) definitions of direct and indirect evidence and applying them to examples for administrative program review, indirect evidence would be the type of data that are collected through means that are designed to gather evidence, such as surveys. Direct evidence is more inherent to the function one is evaluating, such as tracking and reading Web use patterns when students register for courses. While both methods have value when assessing outcomes, some may be more revealing about how the outcomes were met or not met and, thus, may lead to more informed decision making.

For example, a program selects an indirect outcome of "increasing retention rates by 4 percent." Upon measuring that outcome, it learns that retention rates of students who participated in their program did not increase by 4 percent. What do the program faculty and administrators do with that information? How do they improve their program? Or the program administrators may have chosen to engage in direct evaluation methods for outcomes, such as using a scavenger hunt to see whether students can identify two separate offices offering academic support. In this manner, if students are unable to do so, program faculty and administrators know what to improve in the program and may begin to ascertain why these students are not persisting as expected. Selecting evaluation methods that help inform decisions is important, regardless of whether they are direct or indirect means of evaluation.

Whether using direct or indirect outcome measures, selecting multiple methods of evaluation will reveal a better understanding of what was learned about the outcome and will inform more meaningful decisions (Bresciani et al, 2004; Maki, 2004; Palomba & Banta, 1999; Suskie, 2004). Selecting several methods to evaluate one outcome is good research. However, selecting multiple methods for each outcome is something that evolves over time, as faculty and staff become more skilled in embedding outcomes-based assessment into their day-to-day ways of doing.

Selecting evaluation methods for each outcome often requires the assistance of several program faculty and/or administrators. Furthermore, it often takes time to identify an evaluation method that actually provides program faculty and staff with meaningful information they can use to inform decisions for continuous improvement. To emphasize further, both faculty and staff involvement and the selection of the evaluation methods evolves over time. Note the following example from Hampden-Sydney College:

> In 1978, the Hampden-Sydney College Faculty passed the following resolution: "All Hampden-Sydney graduates will write competently." This statement captured the firm conviction of the entire Hampden-Sydney community (faculty, staff, students, alumni, and trustees) that good writing and clear thinking go hand in hand and must be an intrinsic part of our curriculum. Regular assessments of the components of the Program are as important to the work of the Rhetoric staff as is instruction of their students. The program faculty determined that multiple assessments used on a regular basis are necessary because of the complexity of the Program and the demanding multiple levels of requirements for student performance.
>
> The College's writing proficiency requirement consisted of two distinct parts: first, all Hampden-Sydney students must pass two semester-long courses, Rhetoric 101: Principles and Practice of Good Writing I and Rhetoric 102: Principles and Practice of Good Writing II, which both have standard requirements in terms of numbers of pages the students must write and in terms of the final exams they must pass (a timed essay exam and an exam on issues of grammar or style); and second, all Hampden-Sydney students must pass the Rhetoric Proficiency Examination (RPE)

before they may be graduated from the College. Students with weaker backgrounds in writing are offered the opportunity to take Rhetoric 100: Introduction to Grammar and Composition, an elective course that provides them with an extra semester's instruction in writing and grammar. All Rhetoric classes have a 14-student maximum enrollment so that professors may have sufficient time to read and grade their students' essays carefully and so that they may have time to meet with their students in individual conferences at least twice each semester. Despite the relatively large number of sections of rhetoric that the College offers each semester (between 30 and 35), the staff works together to ensure unity of goals for the courses. The staff achieves harmony of purpose by sharing a common text (currently *The Bedford Handbook*), by basing syllabi on a common set of guidelines for each course (students are also given a copy of these guidelines; http://www.hsc.edu/academics/rhetoric/guidelines.html) and by creating and administering common final editing and essay exams.

In one of our assessment projects, program faculty reviewed portfolios for work completed in Rhetoric 102, to make sure that students from different sections of that course were being held to similar standards by various faculty members. In another case, they reviewed a sample of RPEs using a "Primary Trait Analysis" (Herdegen 2002, 2004) approach that the staff designed in order to see where students at that level needed more instruction. [Appendices G-1 and G-2 illustrate two Primary Trait Analysis Scoring Guides used recently.] In one particular case, examining the goal that relates to students' ability to use Standard Written English and their ability to develop their own writing style and voice led the staff to redesign the grammar and editing focus of Rhetoric 102, and to develop an entirely new kind of final exam for editing in that course. They are now in the process of finding ways to assess the effectiveness of that new focus. (Submitted by Elizabeth J. Deis and Earl Fleck, Hampden-Sydney College)

Getting faculty and administrators started in outcomes-based assessment program review may mean that they begin by articulating only one outcome and one evaluation method. The use of multiple methods on multiple outcomes will come in time as they embed this practice into their day-to-day ways of doing.

Subject/Task Being Evaluated

Only 53 percent of the institutions in this study require each program to describe the sample or population being evaluated or require a description of the task or service being evaluated; thus 53 percent reported that the results are somewhat to very important in making decisions for continuous improvement.

While it may not be necessary to report the subject/task that is being evaluated at an institutional level, if it is a large institution, asking program faculty and staff to take the time to identify the sample population of their study may be helpful to institutional coordination of the assessment processes. This is particularly important where students are involved. If this reporting practice occurs, the university assessment committee or professionals can coordinate where certain students are sampled and avoid oversampling of one student population while another sample goes untapped. The Division of Student Affairs at Oregon State University and Texas A&M University discovered that being able to identify who was being evaluated within each assessment plan helped them to coordinate and collaborate administering division-wide student satisfaction surveys as well as facility use practices.

Identification of the sample population for the assessment process also helps in planning administration of the evaluation method. The First Year College at North Carolina State University wanted to use a pre-post test methodology for evaluating transference of learning study skills from one course to another. The college identified all the students in the study skills program and preenrolled those students in a general education course so they could ensure the ability to post-test them at the end of the academic year. It took quite a bit of planning and foresight, but it allowed the college to use the methodology of its choosing because it identified the subjects being evaluated up front.

Results by Outcomes

All but one of the institutions in this study require each program to report a summary of its findings for each outcome evaluated, and, likewise, all but one institution reported that the results are somewhat to very important in making decisions for continuous improvement.

As mentioned in the program and learning outcomes section, many regional and professional accreditors want to be able to identify what has been learned about which outcome. Therefore, while not necessarily required, it may be of great value to report these findings as they relate to program and/

or student learning outcomes. This type of reporting makes clear that faculty and staff have reflected on and planned for the specific results of their doing.

In addition, linking the results back to the program and/or student learning outcomes makes the results less difficult to interpret, so it becomes less challenging to improve your program because you are more confident about which outcomes are being delivered as you desired and which ones need to be refined. An example of this type of reporting results by outcomes follows.

Intended Program Outcomes

1. Assure availability of at least 250 Co-op work listings each semester.

   Findings: Average active per semester 170 Job titles with 267 Positions

   Impact: Due to the economic slowdown, there has been a decrease in job availability. Federal labor projections suggest the possibility of market improvement in the coming year. We will work to improve our position in this area while nurturing our current employer relationships to assure maximum Co-op work listings each semester.

2. Strive to have 200 qualified students apply for Co-op work assignments each semester.

   Findings: 8/02–12/02   213 Applicants
   1/03–05/03   323 Applicants
   6/03–07/03   65 Applicants

   Impact: We were able to reach our goal for qualified applicants. It is our intent to continue the methods used for meeting our goal of 200 qualified students. The fee-based nature of the Co-op program's budget dictates this minimum level of activity.

3. Facilitate a minimum of three interactions between student participants and a Co-op coordinator during their first work rotation.

   Findings: Approximately 87 percent of first-rotation students had three or more interactions during their first work rotations.

   Impact: We would prefer to see this proportion exceed 95 percent. Unfortunately, budget and staffing level constraints limit our ability to visit every out-of-state work site. We will attempt to address these issues in the coming year by seeking to supplement our staff with qualified graduate assistants and by exploring cost effective Web-based solutions for facilitating long-distance coordinator/student interactions.

4. Co-op participants will have a higher persistence to graduation rate than nonparticipants.

Findings: The most recent available data from University Planning and Analysis (UPA) found continuation rates for Co-op participants on average exceeded 99 percent at the three-year mark. This compared with 75 percent for non-participants.

UPA Analysis of graduation patterns disclosed that Co-op participants average a six-year rate of 64 percent, while nonparticipants average 56 percent. The average seven-year rates were shown to be 87 percent for Co-op participants and 62 percent for nonparticipants.

Impact: The data support our assertion that Co-op participation improves university retention and graduation rates. We will continue our efforts in this area. (Submitted by Arnold Bell, North Carolina State University)

Interpretation of Results as They Relate to Outcomes

Similar to the example above, this step requires that interpretation of the results be included, but that the actual results are not necessarily included. All but one of the institutions in this study require each program to report a summary of their interpretation of the findings for each outcome evaluated. Similarly, all but one institution reported that the results are somewhat to very important in making decisions for continuous improvement. An example of this type of assessment report is included below.

Assessment of Outcome 1.b
B.S. in Biomedical Engineering (BME)
May 16, 2003

The second outcome for the first objective was evaluated using two methods (1.b.i. and 1.b.ii.) during two meetings of the BME Courses and Curriculum Committee (CCC). The numbers in parentheses refer to the related criteria (3 and 8) and outcomes (3a–3k) that are specified by ABET for accreditation as an engineering program.

1. To educate students to be successful in Biomedical Engineering by emphasizing engineering and biology as related to basic medical sciences and human health (3a, 3b, 3c, 3e, 3j, 3k, 8)

After completing the B.S. in Biomedical Engineering, students will be able to:

b. Identify contemporary clinical issues and be able to discuss potential biomedical engineering solutions (3a, 3e, 3j, 3k, 8)

i. Written term projects from BAE 382 on selected contemporary human health issues and relevant biomedical engineering solutions. Student understanding of the contemporary issue and its biomedical engineering solutions is assessed by faculty with a faculty-designed rubric. The goal is for 100 percent of BME graduates to achieve this outcome at the competent level as defined by the rubric (every semester the course is taught).

The 47 students in BAE 382: Biomedical Engineering Applications in spring 2003 worked in teams of three or four to develop a WWW-based project on a body system or topic in biomedical engineering.

Student teams were asked to address contemporary issues by addressing the following items:

1. The project must substantively reference at least five peer-reviewed scientific research articles that were published after 1998.
2. The project must identify and clearly articulate one or more opportunities for biomedical engineering solutions of clinical problems.
3. The identified problem must be specific and focused.
4. Solutions should be assessed in terms of timeliness, i.e., urgency and prevalence of the problem.
5. Solutions should be addressed in terms of available technology.
6. The efficacy of current and previous solutions is addressed.
7. The impact on society of proposed solutions is discussed.
8. Statistical information from referenced papers is provided to substantiate the impact on society.
9. The discussion addresses the complexity of issues, including an analysis of the cost/benefit of proposed solutions.

Ten members of the BME CCC met on May 5 and evaluated the BAE 382 WWW-based projects with regard to this outcome. Three committee members evaluated a printed excerpt from each project report in terms of whether it offered evidence of achievement of each of the nine items or not. The excerpt for each project was selected by the course instructor as the segment of the report in which achievement of this outcome should have been evident. A project report was considered to represent competent achievement if at least two committee members indicated that at least six of the nine items had been achieved. Eight of the 12 projects that were evaluated were determined to have met the criteria for competency. The committee made the following recommendations:

a. The literature requirement should be expanded to include recent conference publications in addition to peer-reviewed publications, since conference publications represent the most contemporary work in a given area of biomedical engineering. This modification will be made to the project instructions given to students in spring 2004. All spring 2003 projects were deemed to be competent in this area as it was currently defined.

b. Projects should be evaluated in their entirety after being made available on the WWW rather than from excerpts from the project reports. Three people (Abrams, McCord, and Nagle) were assigned to a subcommittee that will review the four projects that were not considered as representing competent work based on a review of excerpts of the project. In the future, all reviews will be conducted on complete projects rather than excerpts.

The BME CCC will make additional recommendations with regard to this outcome after the members of the subcommittee complete the evaluations of the four remaining projects.

ii. Examples of student answers to exam questions from BAE 382 in which students address the problems associated with the interaction between living and non-living materials. A faculty team identifies exam questions that address this outcome from each of these courses. The scores for each student on each of the selected exam questions are summed and compared to the maximum total possible. The goal is for 95 percent of BME students to achieve 75 percent of the maximum total points (every semester the course is taught).

Exam questions representing a total of 54 points (18 percent of the total for three exams given in BAE 382) were selected as being questions that addressed aspects of the interaction between living and non-living materials. Thirty-seven of the 47 students in the class (78.7 percent) achieved the goal of accumulating 75 percent of the 54-point total.

Before discussing these results, the nine committee members who attended the May 16 meeting voted to raise this item to the level of an outcome. Outcome 1.f., "Discuss the problems associated with the interaction between living and non-living materials (3a, 8)," was added to the outcomes for the first program objective.

After a vigorous discussion, members of the committee decided to adopt a minimum competency criterion, i.e., that 100 percent of the students would accumulate a minimum of 60 percent of the total available points. Forty-six of the 47 students achieved this goal. Subsequent examination of the data indicated that the one student who did not exhibit competency on this outcome was a student with a documented learning disability who chose to take the examinations without taking advantage of the special accommodations that were available to him/her.

The committee made the following recommendations:

a. The course instructor should reevaluate the material in the course and the questions that were asked on the exam to see if there were things that could be done in BAE 382 to improve student learning about the interaction between living and non-living materials. The instructor will be asked to respond to the BME CCC.

b. Future assessments will include student performance in senior level elective courses, e.g., BAE 485, TE 466, and BAE 590I (which has become BME 441 and will replace BAE 522 as an elective), so that more data will be available.

Additional discussion ensued concerning what should be the goal that the program should aim for in terms of this and other outcomes, e.g., 100 percent of the students would achieve 100 percent of the maximum total points, or 95 percent of the students would achieve 75 percent of the maximum total points. Discussions on this issue will continue at future BME CCC meetings as we continue to develop our assessment process.

Previous discussions at BME CCC meetings involved concern on the part of members of the committee that students were not having enough opportunities to learn about the interaction between living and non-living materials. Having only 79 percent of the students accumulate 75 percent of the available points indicates that there is room for improvement. During the 2002–2003 academic year, the BME curriculum has undergone major revisions as a result of the formation of the Department of Biomedical Engineering and the transfer of the B.S. in BME from the Department of Biological and Agricultural Engineering to the BME Department, which is effective with the class of 2006. As part of the discussion concerning what a new curriculum based on the objectives and outcomes of the program would look like, the BME CCC concluded that a revised curriculum should include more opportunities for students to learn about the interactions between living and non-living materials. As a result, the curriculum has been revised to add a biomaterials course in the sophomore year (MAT/BME 203) and to expand the current two-course sequence (BAE 381: Human Physiology for Engineers and BAE 382: Biomedical Engineering

Applications) into a three-course sequence that includes introductory topics in biomedical engineering (BME 202), followed by two courses on human physiology for engineers (BME 301 and BME 302).

Expanding the curriculum to include a four-semester sequence with an additional laboratory in human physiology for engineers in BME 302 should increase student learning in this important area of biomedical engineering. The assessment plan is being rewritten to map the measurement of outcomes to the new courses in the revised curriculum. The criterion for achieving this outcome will be revisited as the assessment plan is revised. (Submitted by Susan M. Blanchard, North Carolina State University)

Decisions and Recommendations Made about the Program for Each Outcome

Eighty percent of the institutions in this study require each program to describe the decisions and recommendations that were made about the program for each outcome evaluated. Eighty percent reported that the results are somewhat to very important in making decisions for continuous improvement.

As a reminder of why this section would be important is the notion that one would want to demonstrate that faculty and staff actually use the information collected from the process to make decisions and recommendations. Some good practice institutions, such as Isothermal Community College and California State University, Sacramento (CSUS), include those decisions in the program review portfolio. Others, such as IUPUI, include the decisions and recommendations made after all of the proper authorities and principal players have discussed the program review portfolio. An example of this type of decision making can be found in the previous section.

Whenever program faculty or staff are having difficulty determining whether they have the authority to make decisions based on the findings from the process that they feel can actually improve their program, making recommendations for improvement may be the wisest thing to do. In other words, when faculty and administrators feel that something is outside their control, such as improvements needed in math courses that are required for their chemistry degree program, recommendations made to the Math Department to make refinements in the math courses may prove optimal for improving their own chemistry program learning outcomes. In making recommendations for improvement, faculty and staff demonstrate the strength and value of the process, while demonstrating accountability to do all they can do to improve their programs and other programs to which they contribute. Furthermore, making recommendations creates an opportunity to use evidence to inform conversations about which improvements can be made collaboratively and why they should be made.

Level of Involvement of Program Faculty/Staff in the Process

Only 67 percent of the institutions in this study require each program to submit a brief description of the program faculty/staff involved at some level in the program review process. Sixty-seven percent reported that knowing this level of involvement is somewhat to very important in making decisions for continuous improvement.

While many institutions and accreditors desire that faculty be involved in the assessment process, gaining faculty involvement is not always easy. Regardless of whether faculty are primarily involved with teaching, research, or service, their involvement in program review is the only way to ensure that the process reflects what the discipline research illustrates the level of quality within the program should be. Without faculty involvement in the process, the meaning and value of decisions will be decreased. For example, when faculty have an opportunity to select what should be evaluated, to discern how it should be evaluated, to deliberate over the findings, they claim ownership of the results generated from the study, so those results can be used to inform decisions for improvement. When faculty are not involved in this process, results are suspect simply because faculty feel detached from the process. When results are suspect, it is less likely that they will inform decisions for improvement.

Jon Wergin (1999) posits that faculty can become involved in the assessment process despite how the process is factored into the institutional rewards structure. He states:

> simply encouraging collaboration is not likely to work; a deeper understanding is needed of faculty preferences. If the unit of assessment is to shift from individual to collective achievement, a different model of motivation is needed. One alternative might be the concept of "organizational motivation," which suggests that faculty members will contribute to the group—even at the expense of self-interest—if they (a) identify with their institution, and (b) think their behavior will affect the institution in a positive way. Thus, rather than focusing all of their attention on "reward

systems," university administrators might be well advised to nurture faculty members' affiliation with the institution, through socialization experiences, ceremonies, and other symbolic acts; by acknowledging faculty whose work benefits the institution; and by removing existing disincentives to participation in institutional citizenship. Administrators might also consider encouraging more discourse about what the institution does and should do for faculty. (p. 1)

An example of this philosophy in action occurs in the following good practice institution:

At University of Wisconsin-Whitewater, faculty input is integral to the audit and review process. A faculty committee reviews the self-study and submits comments to the associate vice-chancellor for academic affairs. The comments are compiled and discussed at a committee meeting. Following the committee meeting, a revised draft is circulated to the committee for its review. The draft report is then sent to the program coordinator, department chair, and dean of the college of the program being reviewed, and a face-to-face meeting is scheduled in which committee members participate. After the meeting, a final report is prepared, and committee members have one more opportunity to review it before it is considered final. Thus, faculty input is included in every step of the audit and review. (Submitted by Richard Telfer, University of Wisconsin-Whitewater)

In this example, faculty can see how they contribute to the decision-making process of program improvement.

Gaining administrative support in program review is often easier as administrators are more accustomed to having tasks assigned to them and complying with administrative directives. However, gaining administrative buy-in to deliberate over assessment results to inform decisions can be tricky if key administrative players are left out of the assessment process loop. Therefore, it is equally as important to involve administrators in programmatic assessment as it is to have pervasive faculty involvement.

In regard to institutions promoting staff involvement in assessment activities, the senior student affairs officers at John Carroll, Oregon State University, Texas A&M University, and all of the Maryland Community Colleges require that their staff engage fully in outcomes-based assessment. Each senior administrator creates a community of expectations around outcomes-based assessment program review, and professional development support is provided to teach staff how to engage in review in a meaningful manner. Position responsibilities include the expectations that assessment will be completed. The Maryland Community Colleges even gather together to articulate outcomes, assessment methods, and instruments they can jointly assess or share among themselves.

To illustrate further, in the Maryland Community Colleges, the senior student services officers have gathered with key individuals from their staff and formulated learning goals that extend across institutions. State government did not require them to come together to articulate learning goals; they simply saw the opportunity that would result. After three years of collaborations, each subunit of each institution has an assessment plan for one of the learning goals that each unit of each institution will contribute to students developing as self-directed learners. While some of the assessment plans' details vary extensively across the units within each college due to varying implementation practices, the learning goals are widely shared and fully embraced. Of all of the hundreds of staff and students involved in assessing this one goal, none of them is promoted for engaging in this activity or receives additional funds to do so. They are getting involved simply because they see the value of demonstrating their day-to-day contributions to student learning (submitted by Cindy Peterka, Maryland Community Colleges).

Time Frame of Evaluation Process

It is probably no surprise that articulating a time frame during which to operate will help ensure that the assessment work is done when you need it (Bresciani et al., 2004). In addition, articulation of a time frame helps keep the program review process manageable. Thus it is no wonder that 73 percent of the institutions in this study require each program to describe a time frame that illustrates who is doing what by when to make sure that the evaluation plan is carried out in a timely manner. Seventy-three percent also reported that knowing the time frame for the evaluation process was somewhat to very important in making decisions for continuous improvement.

At John Carroll University, each unit in the Division of Student Affairs follows the same overall time frame. The assessment cycle at John Carroll takes a full year to complete, beginning July 1 and ending June 30 of the following year. This cycle, in its first year of use, is hallmarked by the following dates and assessment plan requirements:

- July 1, 2004: 2004–05 departmental assessment plans completed
- January 21, 2005: Progress reports that describe the components of the plan undertaken to that point completed
- July 1, 2005: Assessment planning reports that outline plan, describe results, indicate how results will be used to enhance programs and services, and changes to assessment plan for 2005–06 academic year completed
- Cycle starts over (Submitted by Megan Gardner, John Carroll University)

Having such a predefined time frame assists each unit to plan and refine its work further to accommodate the unit's own individual needs and to meet division and institutional reporting expectations.

Another example of a time frame that lends itself well to the academic calendar is that of Texas A&M University:

- Assessment plans for the following academic year (AY) (e.g., 2006–07) are due March of the current AY (e.g., 2006)
  —Assessment plans are reviewed by the appropriate team(s)
- Assessment results of the previous AY (e.g., 2005–06) are due October of the following AY (e.g., 2006)
  —Assessment results are reviewed by the appropriate team(s)

In some cases, it may be important to align the time frames differently for academic programs and administrative programs. It is important to be aware of work cycles and fiscal years for those administrative programs whose reviews may be affected by this. For example, at North Carolina State University, academic support programs with high summer work volume, such as new student orientation, have a different annual assessment reporting cycle from those whose programs are better suited to the academic calendar, such as supplemental instruction.

Furthermore, an institution needs to decide whether it will encourage and support faculty and staff to gather annual assessment data to roll into five-, seven-, or ten-year program review processes, thus decreasing the amount of last-minute preparation for the more comprehensive program review process and making the process much more meaningful and embedded into the day-to-day ways of doing. Some programs within the same institution have different cycles based on their professional accreditation review and their personnel resources. At North Carolina State University, administrative and undergraduate academic program review gathers annual and biannual assessment plans and reports, while graduate program review gathers reports biannually. These assessment plans and reports are reviewed at the point of collection by other faculty who can advise on the quality of the review process. The point is, by the time five years of these annual and biannual reports are rolled up, faculty will have demonstrated increased learning about implementing quality assessment and illustrated improved refinements to their programs. All of this is done to improve the overall quality of higher education, which improves overall student learning.

As referred to in the earlier paragraphs, it is also important to be sensitive to professional accreditation review and standards review cycles. Even if your institution has a ten-year program review cycle, consider being flexible in aligning the program review process with the professional or specialized accreditation cycle of those programs that have external accreditors or standards reviews. Aligning these time frames will make the outcomes-based assessment process more meaningful to the faculty and staff engaged if they can see that their work serves internal institutional accountability purposes as well as professional accreditation or standards review. An excerpt of such a review timetable is found in appendix H.

This type of internal flexibility does require an increased institutional administrative cost early on in the process, as it literally takes more time and effort to educate program faculty and administrators and to provide programs with this type of reporting flexibility. However, the increase in value to those engaged in the outcomes-based assessment program review process may be well worth it.

Support Resources Used

Fifty-three percent of the institutions surveyed require a brief description of the resources used to engage in a meaningful program review process, such as survey methodology, data analysis consultants, and pedagogical consultants. That same percentage reported that knowing the support resources used is somewhat to very important in making decisions for continuous improvement.

Knowing what support resources were used in outcomes-based assessment program review can assist those who support program review in learning more about what is used and how well it contributes to quality review processes. Such knowledge may help in the meta-assessment process and in better understanding what else may be needed to support assessment efforts. Furthermore, identifying these resources may assist with sharing assessment resources and ideas to further promote outcomes-based assessment work.

Plan to Deliver/Implement Outcomes

Sixty percent of the institutions in this study require each program to provide a brief description of the plan that delivered/implemented the evaluated program outcome. Sixty percent reported that knowing of this plan was somewhat to very important in making decisions for continuous improvement.

In the cases where good practice institutions ask programs to outline how services or curriculum are delivered, these institutions demonstrate the link of planning to outcomes-based assessment program review. The linkage of planning for the delivery of a program while planning for its evaluation helps faculty and staff to further identify the value of outcomes-based assessment. In articulating how their program is delivering the intended result, faculty and staff can better identify what that result should be based on their delivery methodology, or they can change their delivery method to better ensure reaching the intended outcome. They can also identify whether they can expect to see the expressed outcome based on whether they are intending to deliver the outcome, and they can identify opportunities inherent to the delivery where there are opportunities to embed evaluation methods.

In some cases, programs plan the delivery in the form of a concept map. See appendix I for an example of this. In other cases, the program gives a summary narrative of how the program is delivering the intended end results. An example from California State University, Sacramento, follows.

> The CSUS collections are in an open stack arrangement that makes the materials directly accessible to CSUS students, with the exceptions of reserve, media, and special collections. With these few exceptions the majority of the collections are physically organized by Library of Congress call number, a nationally accepted library classification scheme that arranges library materials by subject matter. The curriculum collection used by the Teacher Education program is organized by the Dewey classification scheme to replicate the organizational scheme most commonly used in K–12 U.S. school libraries and many public libraries.

The collections also offer different formats to allow for different learning styles. The media collection includes a large collection of 16mm films, audio cassettes, CDs, slides, and videos. Multimedia materials are also part of the Library's curriculum collection. The Library is also providing increasing online access, particularly to reference and journal literature. The online portion of the collection is available 24/7 on campus and from remote sites.

The Library also offers an impressive and growing collection of special collection and archival materials that provide our students primary sources in such areas as regional, state, and national history and politics; social movements; and women's studies.

Include a matrix that displays learning expectations and how courses contribute to achieving the expectations.

Goals	Expectations for Use of Collections	Services to Achieve Expectations
Select Materials	• Develop collections that reflect the breadth and depth of literature in the disciplines • Provide sources that serve to teach students in the use of primary sources for research and study • Provide access to a broad range of information on a subject, from the very general and introductory to the more advanced levels of research • Provide research tools that assist students in learning the research process • Support the development of critical thinking skills through exposure of students to collections that reflect a diversity of perspectives • Provide collections that allow students to trace the evolution of ideas over time and cross-culturally • Provide resources that serve	• Review potential library materials, published and unpublished; current and retrospective; in all formats • Employ criteria for selection decisions, including usefulness to CSUS students, faculty, and staff; applicability to CSUS curriculum; value provided for cost; usefulness of available formats; quality and/or importance of contents; duplication of contents in existing CSUS collection

as teaching tools for CSUS
student teachers
- Support the CSUS academic
faculty in their teaching and
research

Acquire Materials	• Order, receive, and pay for library materials • Receive gifts to the collections • Maintain financial records of library materials purchasing	• Identify and choose vendors to meet library goal of achieving balance between cost and timeliness • Order using best method for individual items, for example, online, procurement card, etc. • Monitor collections budget: supply expenditure information to selectors; prompt orders within the fiscal time frame; notify of overexpenditure • Receive items within a system to maintain financial integrity for auditing purposes • Provide statistics (chancellor, auditor, national agencies) • Serve as point of receipt for gift materials; conduct preliminary search to assist selectors in decision making • Verify that serial/periodical holdings are accurate and received as expected
Manage Collections	• Ensure best access to library materials through online catalog (EUREKA) • Provide accurate holdings for library materials • Provide security for library materials • Preserve library materials • Maintain accurate inventory of the collections • Provide information/instruc-	• Enter bibliographic records for all library materials into EUREKA in which descriptions match the items and access is provided by author/ title/subject and classification • Provide standardized access by name, subject, and series by assuring that only one correct form is used. Provide

tion to reference and instructional faculty on bibliographic matters
- Provide best physical access to library materials
- Provide best physical access for faculty to personal copies of materials
- Provide special access to potential high-use items
- Expand the collection beyond what is owned by the library

cross-references from unused forms to instruct users. This knowledge is transferable to most U.S. academic libraries as well as many other countries
- Assign Library of Congress classification to each item to ensure that similar materials are shelved together. This allows users to browse shelves to find additional items of interest. Familiarity with this classification scheme is transferable to most U.S. libraries as well as those in many other countries
- Keep statistics on the growth of the collection for reporting to state library, chancellor, and for collection development purposes
- Convey information on use of information in bibliographic records as well as rule/form of name or classification changes that may affect access to reference/instruction faculty
- Keep holdings for library materials accurate in EUREKA
- Maintain correct call number order of the collections on the shelves
- Shift collections to provide for growth or reorganization for better access
- Recall checked-out materials for other users; retrieve overdue or missing materials
- Reserve Book Room allows access to high-use materials

		by large numbers of users; provides the opportunity for professors to make personal copies available to students; facilitates access to electronic resources for specific classes
		• Inter Library Loan allows users to borrow materials from other libraries and provides statistics that alert selectors to highly desired materials they should purchase
Assess Collections	See Criteria for Selection above • Assure that library materials continue to reflect the criteria for inclusion in the collections	• Provide ongoing review of the existing collection for currency, continued appropriateness and usefulness to the library's patrons, and lasting value • De-select materials from the collection as needed
Preserve Collections	Protect the collections from damage, aging, theft	• Physical processing of library materials provides some security and preservation for the collections • Provide in-house repair of materials to prolong the life of the collections • Monitor the collections for repair needs during reshelving • Provide security devices at exit portals • Reformat materials to preserve content • Convert formats as technology changes • Preserve the technology necessary to access the content of reformatted materials

(Submitted by Linda Buckley, California State University, Sacramento)

Plan to Deliver/Implement Decisions for Improvement

Sixty-seven percent of the institutions in this study require each program to provide a brief description of the plan to deliver/implement the initiatives recommended to improve the program. Sixty-seven percent reported that knowledge of this plan is somewhat to very important in making decisions for continuous improvement.

When good practice institutions provide this information, they illustrate a desire for faculty and staff to plan for carrying out the recommendation or decision made based on the outcomes-based assessment. In this manner, good practice institutions can identify the cost and priority of the decision's implementation plans if there are many intended changes and not enough resources to make them.

This prioritization can also pose a challenge to institutions that are fully engaged in outcomes-based assessment. Many faculty and staff may demonstrate resistance to engaging in outcomes-based assessment program review for fear that inefficiencies in their programs will be identified, and they will be penalized for these deficiencies. Faculty and staff may become concerned about allocation of resources to address meeting needs they demonstrate through outcomes-based assessment; for example, their program may not be seen as a priority. Not being seen as a resource-worthy priority may cause faculty and staff to resist continuing outcomes-based assessment.

These are valid fears. No institution has enough resources to improve everything that needs to be improved, so hearing that your program is of lower priority is difficult. However, it is better to go to the table to negotiate with evidence of what you are doing well and information about what you need to do better so an informed conversation can take place. In doing so, you encourage decision makers to articulate their values and not to ignore the evidence-based benefits of your program. If documented well, your results cannot be ignored. If resources for improvement cannot be secured, you can manage expectations for outcomes by illustrating that this is all that can be done with available resources. You may choose not to strive for improvement in this area if the necessary resources are not available. While this strategy can be used to make excuses, the point is to focus conversations at the university on using resources wisely to improve the areas that coincide with the university's priorities. Most institutions cannot be in the top ten in all of their academic programs, and this process can help an institution better inform its discussions of what excellence looks like and what can reasonably be attained.

Including the plan to implement decisions for continuous improvement not only demonstrates how the program can be improved and what resources are needed, but also helps administrators better allocate and leverage resources to improve more programs over time. To emphasize this point further, when programs lay out this kind of detail, administrators have to have the "values" conversation about what may be gained from investing in certain programs and whether the established quality in a certain program is good enough. Even though we present good practice institutions in this book, not all of them have reached a point where the evidence and planning for program improvement is so pervasive that outcomes-based assessment can be pointed to for prioritizing allocation and reallocation of all institutional resources.

In time, as more institutions engage in transparent outcomes-based assessment program review and more programs gather increasing amounts of information about what works and what doesn't, faculty and administrators can expect to have data-driven values discussions about what should be improved and what is "good enough." While this may seem to be a frightening practice, it is better to have values conversations informed by data gathered and analyzed by faculty and administrators themselves, rather than uninformed opinions, politically motivated opinions, or opinions formed by meaningless indicators.

Course Syllabi

Fifty-three percent of the institutions in this study require each program to provide a list of the syllabi used in the program review process. The same percentage reported that knowing about the syllabi is somewhat to very important in making decisions for continuous improvement.

Many regional accrediting agencies require that programs list the courses and syllabi they are teaching within the program. Very few require the programs to list activities or workshops that make up their service offerings or research. Fewer still require programs to map or link those courses or activities to program learning outcomes. The value of doing the last, discussed earlier as concept mapping, can assist a program to better plan delivery and evaluation of student learning.

Mapping of Course and Activity Outcomes to Program and Student Learning Outcomes

To illustrate the point further, 40 percent of the institutions require that each program provide a diagram that illustrates the connections between the activity or course that delivers an outcome and then further links the course or activity outcome to the program outcome. To curricular and co-curricular programs, "maps provide an overview of students' learning journey—a place to locate where educational opportunities are specifically designed to address institution- and program-level expectations" (Maki, 2004, p. 38). Mapping course syllabi to demonstrate how courses are delivering and meeting program outcomes helps faculty further identify where and how learning is being delivered and where it needs to be improved. The same process can be used in co-curricular programs. Again, a similar process for linking activities and workshops to program outcomes can be used.

NCATE and ABET require academic programs to map their courses to program outcomes. While no one agency requires co-curricular or administrative programs to map their day-to-day activities to their program outcomes, the benefit of doing so is the same; programs can identify what needs to be improved and what is working well. A practice example of a completed template can be found in appendix I. Such mapping assists in managing expectations of what learning can be expected from a given delivery method.

Miscellaneous

Other items that were included by some, but less than half, of the good practice institutions include the following:

1. **Limitations for Each Evaluation Method.** Only 7 percent of the institutions require that each program list the limitations of each evaluation method. The purpose of including limitations for each evaluation method is to encourage those designing the methods to think about the full design and how to improve it, given the known or perceived limitations of each method. In addition, the limitations help those interpreting the results to do so in a manner that accounts for the limitations of the methodology or to simply acknowledge them and look for them again as they reevaluate the program in the following years.

2. **Targeted Audience.** Thirty-three percent of the good practice institutions require a brief description of the audience targeted to read the program review. Identifying the recipient of the information can often help to formulate the reporting format so that the recipient of the report fully understands what is attempting to be communicated. Identifying the target audience of the self-review report also means that certain types of language can be used to communicate more meaningfully to each audience type, particularly if the recipients of the information have varied expectations, and their inclination is to respond to varying reporting formats.

3. **Plan to Disseminate Results of Review.** Forty percent require each program to include a brief description of the plan to disseminate the results of the review and an illustration of who will be involved in making recommendations based on the results. This is an effective way to illustrate all those who have played a role in formulating the recommendations that arose from outcomes-based assessment program review results. Such documentation illustrates accountability for implementation by listing all those involved in formulating recommendations and decisions. Furthermore, it serves as a helpful referral when clarification is needed for recommendations and interpretation of results.

4. **Summary of the Review Process.** Forty-seven percent require each program to include a summary of how well the review process worked for them. While only 47 percent of the good practice institutions require this, Sinclair Community College reported that the description of the self-study process was helpful in understanding the department's status and preparation for the program review. The description also informs the institution about the strengths of the overarching process and provides information about what the department would do differently in the next review cycle.

5. **Decisions and Recommendations Made about the Review Process.** Forty percent of the institutions in the survey require each program to include a summary of the decisions and recommendations they have made to improve the next review process. Doing so allows programs to identify how they can improve a process that is helping them improve their programs. For example, Isothermal Community

College reports that the act of reporting decisions and recommendations about the review process has led it to enact a "culture shift" by including assessment language and references to its campuswide rubrics in course syllabi. The college also published all the criteria and rubrics in a handout for students and began to include an assessment and student portfolio session in its success and study skills (new student orientation) class. In addition, it added an assessment vocabulary list to the student handbook so students could better understand the process as well.

6. **Faculty/Staff Development.** Thirty-three percent of the institutions surveyed require each program to provide a brief description of the faculty and staff development that was initiated to complete the review process. To emphasize the learning nature of engagement in outcomes-based assessment program review, some good practice institutions encourage the program to plan for how they will educate faculty and staff to improve their programs. Other good practice institutions have an institution-wide faculty and staff development plan or partner with specific units on campus, such as the faculty development center or human resources, to deliver the required education. One example of a comprehensive faculty and staff development plan can be found at http://assessment.tamu.edu/StrategicPlanning forEBDM.html.

7. **Student Portfolios.** Thirteen percent of the institutions require each program to submit a brief description of or referral to the portfolios maintained by students as a tool for reflection on the learning process and their experiences. Alverno College requires the use of individual student portfolios in its program assessment process. While Truman State University does not require the use of portfolios, the random sampling of such portfolios provides a useful reflection of student learning achievements for the program as a whole.

8. **External Review.** Forty-seven percent of the institutions require each program to submit a listing of individuals external to the institution who are reviewing the program and process. At IUPUI, "members of visiting teams, who usually spend 2½ days on campus following their review of a self-study prepared by the unit, include two or three disciplinary specialists from outside Indiana, a community stakeholder

with interests in the area being reviewed, and two IUPUI colleagues from related units. The entire team can be helpful in recommending improvements in teaching and learning, scholarship and research, civic engagement, commitment to diversity, and pursuit of best practices. In addition, the community representative provides an invaluable perspective on the unit's civic engagement, while the internal colleagues can assist particularly in assessing the unit's current collaborative efforts and in suggesting future opportunities for cross-disciplinary work." (Submitted by Trudy Banta and Karen Black, IUPUI)

Texas A&M University Division of Student Affairs reports that they

> have on-campus external reviewers (one reviewer from outside the program but within the Division and one reviewer from outside the Division but within the University). The on-campus external reviews, like the off-campus external reviews, have four goals:
>
> 1. to provide an objective, unbiased view of the program's strengths, weaknesses, opportunities, and current or potential areas of concern;
> 2. to provide focused feedback concerning the program's connections to the University's liberal arts and sciences mission;
> 3. to critique the program's process of continuous quality improvement;
> 4. to highlight student learning and effective teaching; and to encourage an exchange of ideas, methods, etc., between reviewers and faculty, staff, and students, making the review a worthwhile experience for all. (Submitted by Sandi Osters, Texas A&M University)

California State University, Monterey Bay, also requires use of a member external to the program being reviewed to question the program administrators and faculty about issues of student learning.

1. **Use of Benchmarking Indicators or Tools such as the National Survey of Student Engagement (NSSE).** One-third of the institutions require each program to submit a brief description of any tools or processes used to compare services, products, and processes based on best practices and/or preexisting programs. While only one-third of the good practice institutions require this, John Carroll University

reports that in addition to the departmental assessment plans, the Division of Student Affairs engages in myriad assessment processes that contribute to a comprehensive body of knowledge about the student experience. The following national survey instruments are used to provide additional information about the university's students:

- Cooperative Institutional Research Program (CIRP) Freshman Survey
- Your First College Year (YFCY) Survey
- College Student Survey (CSS)
- Educational Benchmarking Institute Resident Satisfaction Survey (RSS)
  Educational Benchmarking Institute Resident Assistant Satisfaction Survey (RASS)
- National Survey of Student Engagement (NSSE)
- Faculty Survey of Student Engagement (FSSE)
- Information garnered from these instruments is used to improve programs and services and to enhance the overall student learning process.

2. **Budget for Assessment Project.** Thirty-three percent of the institutions require each program to provide a brief explanation of the established budget for the program review process (e.g., incentives, materials, office supplies). While this may seem to be an obvious item to ask for when requesting an assessment plan, many good practice programs do not ask for this because they expect that outcomes-based assessment budgeting will be a part of the overall program budget. In addition, it is sometimes difficult to separate the budget for evaluating student learning from the instructional cost budget. For example, if one of the evaluation methods is the project you are requiring for the course, should that item be included in the instructional cost budget or the assessment budget? Likewise, some administrative programs have difficulty separating the cost of evaluating their services from the cost of delivering their services, as the assessment practices are so deeply embedded in the day-to-day. Some institutions require a separate budget if the program calls for a comparative analysis that necessitates purchasing benchmarking tools or if the program is using

external evaluators when none is typically required or is not furnished from the central institutional program review budget.

3. **Budget to Deliver/Implement Outcomes.** Thirteen percent of the institutions require a brief explanation of the established budget for delivery of the program outcomes that were evaluated (e.g., incentives, staff, materials, office supplies). Here, institutions request that programs outline the budget (and, often, the plan) for delivering the outcome. This is done to ensure that proper funding for the expected implementation practice or project has been planned. The intent is that the decision and recommendation resulting from the assessment results may then be more successful because there is a plan to fund their implementation.

4. **Budget to Deliver/Implement Decisions for Improvement.** Twenty percent of the institutions require a brief explanation of the proposed budget for delivery of the recommended improvements (e.g., incentives, staff, materials, office supplies). The budget proposed in this step is done to help decision makers prioritize budget allocations and reallocations to the improvements recommended by outcomes-based assessment. If all programs are engaged in outcomes-based assessment, most institutions do not have the resources to improve all programs. Therefore, having the results, recommendations, plans for improvement, and estimated costs of those improvements helps decision makers determine which improvements can be funded and when. It is, indeed, a very informed manner in which to allocate program and institutional resources.

5. **Activity/Workshop Programs.** Twenty percent of the institutions require a listing of the activity/workshop programs used in the program review process. Similar to requiring syllabi for academic program review, administrative units may want each program to provide a listing of its programs and workshops that are designed to help the program deliver its outcomes.

6. **Curriculum Vitas for Faculty/Resumes of Staff.** Forty-seven percent of the institutions require a listing of curriculum vitas for program faculty and resumes of program staff to be included in the program under review. Some good practice programs require curriculum vitas for program faculty and resumes of program staff so they can evaluate

the expected competencies for delivering specific outcomes in programs. Others indicate that this activity may be a holdover from accreditation requirements in the days when faculty and staff vitas were not readily accessible via the Web.

7. **Inputs Assessment Requirements.** Since this study focused on outcomes-based assessment, questions were not posed to all of the good practice institutions about their use of inputs assessment data in program review processes. However, institutions such as IUPUI, North Carolina State University, Truman State University, and Texas A& M University report using data gathered by various institutional surveys, as well as entering students statistics, to plan particular programs, especially for specific subpopulations, such as that of Truman State's plan for academic support interventions for students. See http://assessment.truman.edu/grants/2004/development%20and %20assessment%20of%20an%20early%20identification%20model .htm for details.

Another good practice example is how Student Life Studies at Texas A&M University shares incoming characteristics of students with faculty and staff so they can expect particular attitudes in the classroom. Some of these attitudes and perceptions have been used to modify the delivery of educational and student support programs so students are better equipped to transition to the culture and academic rigor of that institution.

Outcomes-based academic program review is a "thinking person's process" (T. Benberg, December 7, 2003). In essence, it requires faculty and co-curricular professionals to purposefully plan the delivery of the intended student learning as well as systematically evaluate the extent to which that learning has been met and to propose recommendations for improving delivery of the learning. Thus, outcomes-based program review requires faculty to engage in conversations around what they want students to be able to know and to do and then intentionally plan a program that delivers and evaluates that learning. The same is true for research and service—all must be purposefully articulated, planned, delivered, and evaluated. Thus, the intentional conversation for how this is done is one of the goals for outcomes-based program review, and it will evolve as the institution evolves in what it learns from engaging in outcomes-based program review. As Alverno College states,

Over time, the review practices at Alverno College have developed in different directions, while still addressing similar commitments to educational quality. In our case, program review implements a continuous improvement philosophy naturally embedded in the course and external assessment process, whereby faculty are continually aware of student performance and deliberate on it at the department level based on their shared responsibility for program outcomes. In this context:

- A range of review and inquiry processes is integrated into practice, addressing different programmatic topics as appropriate and needed; taken together for particular venues (e.g., an accreditation report), these can constitute a more traditional definition of program review.
- The primary medium of review is discourse and deliberative inquiry based on evidence of student performance and educational practice; consequently, reporting per se may come in a variety of forms, ranging from written reports to presentations to structured dialogues.
- Procedures for dissemination, decision making, planning, and implementation develop from the operational structure, so that key stakeholders are typically the primary audience for inquiries, and then the discourse moves across different levels and units.
- Support dimensions for these practices (e.g., budget and faculty development) are embedded and diffused through the campus.
- As an overall practice of review, the emphasis is on a coherent system guided by policies and practices that have evolved gradually out of shared experience rather than on a specified set of ingredients.
- Recurring documentation provided by departments, committees, and work groups (including minutes, process documents, and reports) becomes a critical source of data for deliberative inquiry and is used periodically as a basis for critiquing and articulating educational principles out of practice. (Submitted by Marcia Mentkowski, Alverno College)

While it may be discouraging or encouraging to read about Alverno's own evolution as a learning community, keep in mind that Alverno College has been intentionally engaged in self-review for almost thirty years. Its level of sophistication is, indeed, a good practice. It will, as will all of these good practice institutions, tell you that it didn't start out where it is today. The source of what the school now has, as mentioned, has been decades of improving upon its own self-reflection process until it has become embedded into the day-to-day practices of faculty and staff. For more details of Alverno College's Outcomes-Based Assessment Program Review, see appendix J.

As a reminder, the purpose of this book is not to provide you with a clean set of "to dos" so you can go back to your institution and "plug everyone and everything in"; the point of this book is to provide you with various frameworks and examples so your institution can approach program review with shared reflection. If everyone in an institution does not engage in outcomes-based program review with similar (not necessarily same) intentions, then the practice of outcomes-based program review and the use of the results gained from the practice may be done incorrectly or not at all. In addition, it is important to emphasize that while institutions may share frameworks for outcomes-based program review, the adopting institution must be able to apply that framework within its own institutional culture. Doing so allows the institution to engage in genuinely meaningful dialogue about what the institution is learning about student leaning in the context of its own institutional values.

4

CRITERIA FOR GOOD PRACTICES OF OUTCOMES-BASED ASSESSMENT PROGRAM REVIEW

This chapter examines the criteria on which the evidence of effective outcomes-based assessment is founded. As we discussed earlier, the primary purpose of outcomes-based assessment program review is for faculty and co-curricular programs to engage in a systematic, reflective process that allows them to gather evidence to improve their programs. So, for an outcomes-based assessment program to be effective, criteria for defining "effective" need to be applied to the program review process and evaluation to determine whether the process in place is resulting in increased reflection, data gathering, and decisions for improvement.

The following discussion presents the results of the good practice institutions' survey responses and case studies. As discussed earlier, we organized the criteria into categories informed by the research of Cecilia Lopez (1997, 2002), Peggy Maki (2004), Banta (2002), Palomba and Banta (1999), Ewell and Jones (1996), Eder (1999), and the American Association of Higher Education's (1994) *Nine Principles of Good Practice for Assessing Student Learning*.

It is important to note that all of the good practice institutions do not evaluate their program review processes in the same manner. Thus, using the following criteria to evaluate your institution's outcomes-based assessment program review process must be done with care. As we stressed in the preceding chapter, each institution must determine the most effective way to implement and evaluate its outcomes-based assessment process. These criteria serve only as a guide. An example of one institution's application of these criteria in its evaluation process can be found at http://www.ncsu.edu/provost/academic_programs/uapr/assess/assessment_of_assessment.html.

In addition, application of the criteria and their values varies by institutional type and culture, so it will also vary as you apply it to your own institutional program review process. Furthermore, just as outcomes-based assessment program review is an iterative process (Maki, 2004), so is evaluation of the process itself. Therefore, as you implement outcomes-based assessment program review or refine what your institution already has in place, keep in mind that you may be able to demonstrate some of the following characteristics fully, yet may not be able to demonstrate others of them at all. The point is to keep the program review process genuine and meaningful and progress along with good practices as you are able so that your process of purposeful reflection, evaluation, and decision making will be enduring, effective, and efficient.

As mentioned earlier, no two good practice institutions approach outcomes-based assessment program review exactly the same way. Steps to implementing outcomes-based program review vary, templates for outcomes-based assessment and program review guidelines vary, and, therefore, where these institutions place themselves within the criteria for good practices varies as well. Similarly, institutions may choose not to comply with all of the criteria for evaluating good practice outcomes-based assessment program review.

Explanation of and education about the outcomes-based assessment program review process, while often presented as a linear process, is not linear at all (Bresciani et al., 2004). The following criteria are discussion points to enable you to evaluate how well your institution is progressing toward meaningful and manageable systematic outcomes-based assessment program review. Because the process is not at all linear, you may find your institution moving forward in some categories and backward in others. This is a dynamic process that requires flexibility, tolerance of ambiguity, and a constant commitment to genuine reflection that resonates from program faculty and staff.

Criterion 1: Clear Understanding of Goals and Expectations for Program Review

Bresciani and associates (2004), Maki (2004), and Palomba and Banta (1999) state that institutions must have a clear understanding of goals and expectations for program review. If faculty and co-curricular professionals do not understand the purpose of outcomes-based assessment program review, they cannot recognize its value and will not be able to meaningfully engage in its practice (Rodrigues, 2002; Wergin, 1999). Furthermore, communicating the value and importance of outcomes-based assessment in a manner in which faculty and staff can then articulate it well is also a criterion for good practice institutions.

All of the good practice institutions in this study reported that it is somewhat to very important that faculty and administrators across the institution have a clear understanding of the goals and objectives for program review, and that faculty and administrators across campus are able to articulate a level of understanding of the institution's program review process. In other words, faculty and staff have to understand that this is not a process for process's sake; it is, rather, a commitment to intentionally improve student learning and the many facets that support it. That is the point of it all. At Alverno College, underlying principles for program review are made very clear. Program review exists to

- build a community of scholarship and practice in which program review has an organic role and informs educational practice and decisions;
- build the infrastructure that will sustain the related practices (e.g., leadership, budgets, training, and support);
- infuse empirical study of student learning outcomes into pedagogical, curriculum, and program planning and decisions;
- align governance, curriculum, teaching practices, and a commitment to student learning in the campus culture (e.g., promotion and tenure that recognizes faculty efforts in program review and the application of policy results);
- instigate dialogue—within the academic community, with the public, with boards, with legislators, and so on; and
- increase participation in service of student learning outcomes.

Sinclair Community College makes the purpose of its outcomes-based assessment program review very clear in its guiding principles (see http://www.sinclair.edu/about/assessment/principles/index.cfm).

Students' role in outcomes-based assessment program review remains the subject of debate at many institutions. For example, at Alverno College, students play a key function in program evaluation, as their reflection on their abilities is key to informing faculty conversations about needed improvements in curriculum design. At North Carolina State University, some academic programs include students in articulating its academic program's learning outcomes. Most good practice institutions agree that students should be able at least to understand what program review is about and what the intended program outcomes mean. Eighty-seven percent of the institutions reported that it is somewhat to very important that *students* across the institution have a clear understanding of the goals and objectives of program review. Eighty-seven percent of the institutions also reported that it is somewhat to very important for *students* to understand the outcomes articulated for each program.

It is often said that people spend their time based on what they value (Covey, 1989). If this is true, then it is increasingly important to help faculty recognize the link between their outcomes-based assessment program work and research and core educational practices (Maki, 2004; Rodrigues, 2002; Wergin, 1999). Eighty-seven percent of the good practice institutions reported that it is somewhat to very important that academic programs consider program review integral to their educational and research operations.

In addition, if you visit with faculty and administrators on your campus, you will most likely find that they are looking for affirmation, both verbal and written, of what the institutional leadership values. Ninety-three percent of the good practice institutions reported that it is somewhat to very important that expectations for assessment be articulated clearly by the president of the institution. Seventy-three percent of the institutions reported that it is somewhat to very important that university publications articulating expectations for program review be shared universally across the institution, while 93 percent of the institutions reported that it is somewhat to very important for university publications articulating expectations for *student learning* to be shared universally across the institution. Keystone College acknowledges the importance of assessment and evaluation in its Vision Statement for the 2004–2008 Strategic Plan.

Keystone College: Vision Statement

By the Fall of 2008, Keystone College will have fully developed the identity, systems, processes, and culture of a Baccalaureate (General) college, while continuing to support selected Associate and transfer programs.

To achieve this, the College will have re-dedicated itself to its Mission and the Keystone Promise, and *will have developed a stable organizational structure that incorporates periodic, cyclical review and evaluation across the campus* [emphasis added]. (For more information on Keystone's process refer to http://styluspub.com/resources/outcomes-basedprogramreview .aspx.)

Determining which institutional leaders and which publications are most important in emphasizing the key role of outcomes-based assessment program review to focus the institution on enacting its values and to determine the extent to which it is achieving those values should be determined by the institution. The point here is that most faculty and staff will not reallocate their time to embedding outcomes-based assessment program review into their day-to-day activity if the leaders they respect do not recognize its value.

Similar to communicating expectations for engaging in outcomes-based assessment and having those expectations become pervasive, one should also be able to articulate the consequences of a program's decision *not* to engage in outcomes-based assessment program review (Bresciani et al., 2004). Ninety-three percent of the institutions reported that it is somewhat to very important that faculty and administrators know the answer to the question, "What happens if I don't engage in assessment?" If faculty and administrators don't know the answer to this question, they may resist or have difficulty allocating time to assessment. For example, faculty know the consequences of not teaching or publishing. However, do they know what happens if they do not choose to articulate learning outcomes, evaluate those outcomes, and reflect on the evidence to make appropriate decisions and recommendations? Is reaffirmation from their professional or institutional accrediting agency at risk? Is funding from their college or division at risk? What are the consequences of not participating in outcomes-based assessment program review? Have they been made clear?

Finally, many institutions struggle with the question of how many of their programs they should evaluate. While many engaged in external accountability conversations may want the answer to be 100 percent, 87 percent of the good practice institutions reported that it is somewhat to very important that there be 100 percent participation in institutional program review efforts. Why did 100 percent of the institutions not expect 100 percent participation?

Some of the reasons for not expecting 100 percent participation have to do with the fact that many new faculty and administrators do not know how to conduct outcomes-based assessment program review. That means that when an institution hires these faculty and staff, they need to be educated about how to evaluate programs in a meaningful manner. (In higher education, we need to pay close attention to orienting new faculty toward this practice until we can expect graduate preparation programs to teach faculty and staff how to do outcomes-based assessment program review.) While many institutions have faculty coming in and out and may also have leadership turnover in programs, the challenge of keeping 100 percent of your faculty and administrators educated about outcomes-based assessment program review may correlate directly with your institution's ability to evaluate 100 percent of its programs. Over time, and as outcomes-based assessment program review becomes more pervasive, it may be that we can expect 100 percent compliance by 100 percent of the institutional faculty and staff.

More important than counting the number of people involved in outcomes-based assessment program review may be keeping the intent and purpose of involvement clear. The point is that the more faculty and administrators are involved in articulating program outcomes, evaluating the results, interpreting the results, and using them to make decisions, the clearer the purpose of program review will become. The clearer the purpose becomes, the more faculty and administrators will become involved as they realize that their expertise is valued in improving their programs. This logic leads to the second criterion.

Criterion 2: Collaboration

Collaboration across faculty and administrative lines is of great value to good practice institutions. Specifically, 100 percent of the institutions reported that it is somewhat to very important that academic colleges and co-curricular departments collaborate with each other to promote the program assessment efforts and process. Eighty-seven percent of the institutions reported that it is somewhat to very important for various faculty and administrators across campus to meet to review the program review process collaboratively and make recommendations for its improvement.

One hundred percent of the institutions reported that it is somewhat to very important for *department outcomes* generated from program review to be shared across the appropriate college/division, and 93 percent reported that it was somewhat to very important for *program review findings* to be shared across the appropriate college and division. Finally, 100 percent of the institutions reported that it was somewhat to very important for faculty and administrators to work together to create program review processes.

At Texas A&M University, a collaborative team of faculty and administrators defined the process for university-wide assessment, the conceptual framework, common language, and templates for outcomes-based assessment program review (see http://assessment.tamu.edu/ScholarshipofAssessmentThinkTank.html for details). Indiana University–Purdue University Indianapolis (IUPUI) also gathered faculty and administrators together to formulate its university-wide processes. In Maryland, student affairs divisions from each community college across the state joined together on their own initiative and began to discuss statewide learning principles that each one of their campuses shared.

At Isothermal Community College, institution-wide outcomes-based assessment efforts emerged out of the academic unit efforts, while at Oregon State and John Carroll, the initiatives arose out of student affairs. Collaborations among several administrative units and grant-funded programs at North Carolina State University helped get an undergraduate outcomes-based assessment program review off the ground and led to further collaborations with the offices of Business and Finance, Student Affairs, and the Graduate School. Regardless of their starting point, all of these good practice institutions would attest to the fact that their efforts are as successful as their collaborations.

A specific example of administrators and faculty collaborating to develop and assess a program follows:

Texas A&M: The Leadership Living Learning Community

The Leadership Living Learning Community at Texas A&M University is a partnership between the Department of Agricultural Education and the Department of Residence Life. It is an opportunity for sixty to one hundred freshmen at Texas A&M University to interact with faculty, staff, and peers as members of a Living Learning Community with a focus on leadership development. The students will live together in Aston and Mosher halls.

In the fall semester of the first year, freshmen complete a one-semester-credit-hour course in leadership development centered on the Tuckman/Jensen Model, using Bennis and Goldsmith's *Learning to Lead, A Workbook on Becoming a Leader.* Co-curricular activities, including field trips and in-residence hall programming, will follow the topics by textbook chapter design. In the spring, the students complete an additional one-semester-credit-hour course in leadership development centered on peer mentoring (student development/leadership theory). In the fall semester of their second year, the sophomores will serve as peer mentors and complete a three-semester-credit-hour course (AGED 340) in professional leadership development. In the spring, the peer mentors complete a two-semester-credit-hour course (AGED 301) in personal leadership development.

The expected outcomes for this program are that students will:

- Understand the positive effects of academic and co-curricular integration
- Communicate the effects of the Group Decision Model
- Integrate leadership theory into their own leadership aspirations
- Assess their own and others' leadership potential
- Connect and use assessment techniques to enhance personal leadership strategies
- Understand the value of self-learning through theory and practice
- Use peer mentoring as an effective example of leader/follower relationships (Submitted by the Learning Community Task Force at Texas A&M University)

Collaboration takes time and comes in many forms. While these examples illustrate cross-divisional line collaborations, there are also examples of collaborations within departments. At several good practice institutions, senior faculty may take the bulk of writing the review to free junior faculty seeking tenure to contribute ideas for program outcomes and plans for improvement.

While some departmental promotion and tenure (P&T) policies may not lend themselves readily to promoting collaborative processes among faculty to improve student learning through outcomes-based assessment program review, there are many ways in which faculty can refine existing policies to have their participation in collaborative learning projects, curriculum reviews and refinements, and course-based assessment count within the promotional area of teaching (Bresciani, Jenefsky, & Wolff, in press). Other institutions count collaborative program review processes in the service portion of the P&T portfolio. Some disciplines considered the published research of collaborative improvements in student learning as scholarship for the research area of the P&T conversations.

Collaboration of all types takes time to embed into day-to-day activities. It also takes departmental acceptance of collaborative work (Bresciani et al., in press). As discussed, collaboration takes many forms. Without it, systematic improvement is difficult to generate and even more difficult to sustain.

Criterion 3: Use of Results

Many institutions tend to focus too much on the process and forget that what they are trying to accomplish is to use the results from the outcomes-based assessment program review to improve student learning and development, research, and service. Therefore, using the results is integral to evaluating whether the process is effective, valuable, and meaningful. Attention to criterion 3 is crucial to evaluating the success of your outcomes-based assessment program review process.

This is so much so the case that 100 percent of the institutions reported that it is very important that results from the program review be used to inform *program* discussions, decisions, and recommendations, while 93 percent thought it is somewhat to very important that results from the program review be used to inform *department* discussions, decisions, and recommendations. One hundred percent of the institutions reported that it is somewhat to very important to use the results from the program review to inform *college/division* discussions, decisions, and recommendations, and 100 percent of the institutions reported that it is somewhat to very important to use results from the program review to inform *institutional* discussions, decisions, and recommendations.

The lower percentage reporting importance in use for departmental decisions may be due to the varying degrees that faculty and administrators agree that their departmental structures are organized in a manner that is conducive to program improvement discussions. In other words, departments typically are organized for administrative purposes. There may be a number of reasons programs of all types are prearranged into the departments in which they reside. Categorizing programs into departments may not be done in a manner that is most helpful to interpreting information and making decisions for improvement at the department level.

Using the results to make recommendations or decisions to improve programs is at the heart of outcomes-based assessment program review. Regardless of how an institution is organized, it must engage in conversations that inform decisions and recommendations for improvement. It may often be the case that due to organizational structure, a program can only make recommendations for improvement as actual decision-making authority may lie outside a program's control (Bresciani et al., 2004). Not using the results of outcomes-based assessment program review, however, defeats its primary purpose; therefore, regardless of organizational structure, recommendations that are informed by evidence can inform those in authority of needed improvements.

Within the criterion of "Use of Results" are several subcategories that can clarify the meaning behind "Use of Results." We explain these subcategories below.

Course Improvement

Ninety-three percent of the institutions reported that it is somewhat to very important for program review outcome findings to be used to make informed decisions in the design and delivery of courses. The majority of good practice institutions report using findings in this manner, yet they emphasize that this cannot be done without knowing how program outcomes depend on the intended outcomes of particular courses and co-curricular experiences. Course or project mapping is of great importance when linking program findings to recommended improvements in courses or projects (Maki, 2004). In addition, many good practice institutions report that doing so also allows faculty and staff to see clearly how program review can improve their day-to-day processes, so they find the most meaning in engaging in this practice, because it directly relates to their day-to-day ways of doing.

One hundred percent of the institutions reported that it is somewhat to very important for key decision makers to meet and discuss the findings and recommendations made through the program review process and for program review results to be used to inform pedagogical decisions in the classroom. A specific example of this type of improvement follows:

Keystone College: Sport and Recreation Management Program

The Sport and Recreation Management program began as an associate degree program. When Keystone became a baccalaureate institution, this program was noted as one that could be expanded to a Bachelor of Science degree. A preliminary sequence of courses was proposed for the upper levels of the major, accepted by the College's Academic Committee, and the baccalaureate program began to enroll students. This gave the Curriculum Coordinator time to develop the content of the 300- and 400-level classes while students were completing the 100- and 200-level courses. Each of these individual courses was designed and accepted by the Academic Committee as well.

The Curriculum Coordinator used the dialectic modality of Keystone's academic structure to develop the sequence and content of the courses in the major, and this dialectic approach comes strongly into play in her ongoing program review. Even as the program was moving its first class of baccalaureate students through the sequence of courses, the Curriculum Coordinator was beginning to review and refine the major. The timing was such that this effort basically coincided with the College's decennial Middle States Self-Study, and that ongoing project made the campus highly aware of the needs of well-stated goals and objectives in many areas. The Curriculum Coordinators of all programs were asked to articulate goals and objectives for their programs.

Starting with the College's General Education Goals and Objectives, the Sport and Recreation Management Curriculum Coordinator drafted a set of goals and objectives specifically for her program that incorporated the General Education concepts as much as possible. She then worked through each of the existing syllabi for the courses in the program to note which General Education Goals and Objectives were addressed in each one. She then went back and forth among all of the syllabi and her own draft of program goals and objectives and completed the same kind of analysis.

This process gave the Curriculum Coordinator an excellent opportunity not only to bring her courses very carefully into alignment with stated goals and objectives, it also allowed her a clarity of vision that helped her refine those goals and objectives.

Continuing to use this dialectic modality, the Curriculum Coordinator was able to work through all of the basic syllabi and course descriptions in her program with a critical eye. The back-and-forth dialectic addressed the questions of "What *exactly* does this assignment/unit do to help the students achieve which objective?" and "Where *specifically* do my program goals and objectives fit into the General Education goals and objectives of the College?" Because of the back-and-forth nature of the inquiry, the Coordinator was able to refine and develop assignments that were clear in their fulfillment of objectives, while also discarding certain assignments that were vague or simply "busy work" and did not advance students toward the goals.

Reviewing students' portfolios as they were developed was also a significant part of the Curriculum Coordinator's program review. By assessing the strengths and weaknesses of early graduates, she was able to go back into the dialectic with syllabi and objectives and determine the best course and time to emphasize and reemphasize necessary skills.

When this review of the Sport and Recreation Management major was complete, the Curriculum Coordinator had a set of refinements to the major ready for the Academic Committee. which reviewed and passed them.

Now, after significant refinement of the major, the Curriculum Coordinator is able to take the annual requirements of the College's End of Year Reports and complete a "mini-version" of what she did before each year.

The College has implemented the use of End of Year Reports to encourage Curriculum Coordinators to engage in the kind of ongoing program review that Sport and Recreation Management did, to use the dialectical modality of our academic structure to strengthen their programs and to strengthen the outcomes of those programs.

Not all curricula have completely embraced this modality yet, but the understanding and development continues with our program development and the evolution of Keystone College into a full Baccalaureate General college. (Submitted by Sherry Strain, Keystone College)

Results Available to the Public

Seventy-three percent of the institutions reported that it is somewhat to very important that results from the program review process be available to the public. At John Carroll University, national survey results are shared with the campus community twice a semester via a publication produced by the Vice President for Student Affairs Office, *What We Know About Our Students*. A second publication, *FOCUS*, distributed to the campus community once a semester, provides information about a specific topic or current issue in higher education, such as minority student retention, student use of technology, or drug and alcohol issues. Information in this publication comes from numerous sources, including departmental assessment results, national and local surveys, higher education literature, focus groups, and interviews. Both publications provide outlets for sharing with the campus community important information that may enhance or inform programming, services, and student learning and development opportunities.

IUPUI makes the results of its program review process public in the form of an online institutional portfolio (see http://www.iport.iupui.edu). This public portfolio provides IUPUI with internal and external accountability about how it defines and evaluates excellence and uses the information to inform decisions and recommendations for improvement.

Sharing results and using results in a public manner further emphasizes the value of outcomes-based assessment program review. In addition, it provides a level of public scrutiny unavailable when program review portfolios sit on dusty bookshelves. Thus, the motivation to engage in a process that actually results in action increases if faculty and administrators know that they have to answer for how decisions are made or if they have to live with the decisions they make based on particular evidence.

However, as is the case with all of these criteria, an institution must pay particular attention to its culture. If public availability of assessment plans and results means that a program will be less likely to gather data or report its results objectively, then public disclosure should be delayed until communities of trust can be established. Public disclosure of assessment plans, results, and decisions means public scrutiny of what they contain. Many institutions cannot take this step until they have established a culture of trust around use of the data and around the process of making recommendations and decisions with that data.

Faculty and Staff Involvement

Eighty-seven percent of the institutions reported that it is somewhat to very important for teams of faculty to be educated to assess the quality of the program review content, while 93 percent reported that it is important to have teams of administrators educated to assess the quality of the program review content.

At University of Wisconsin-Whitewater, faculty input is integral to the audit and review process. A faculty committee reviews the self-study and submits comments to the associate vice-chancellor for academic affairs. The comments are compiled and discussed at a committee meeting, following which a revised draft is circulated to the committee for its review. The draft report is then sent to the program coordinator, department chair, and dean of the college of the program being reviewed, and a face-to-face meeting is scheduled, in which committee members participate. After that meeting, a final report is prepared, and committee members have one more opportunity to review it before it is considered final. Thus, faculty input is included in every step of the audit and review.

Similar to criteria 1 and 2, this subcategory illustrates that involvement of faculty and staff is important in every step of the process. When discussing the use of results, extensive involvement encourages ownership of successes and failures (Palomba & Banta, 1999). When decisions and recommendations are made based on results of outcomes-based assessment program review, staff and faculty can be involved. Various levels of expertise and perspectives can improve interpretation of data and resulting decisions. Furthermore, motivation for involvement is often higher when results are introduced, as people begin to see that something will actually be done with the planning conversations that preceded data collection. Furthermore, the Council of Regional Accrediting Commissions (CRAC) document of 2003 highly encourages faculty involvement in the student learning assessment process.

Informing Performance Indicators

Sixty percent of the institutions reported that it is somewhat to very important for program review results to inform interpretations of global performance indicators such as those from *U.S. News and World Report* or those from the state legislature. With growing demand from the public to quickly understand and compare the quality of education among several universities, rankings such as those of *U.S. News and World Report* have been formulated. Unfortunately, such rankings typically lack any meaningful interpretation of actual quality of student learning, research, or service. Therefore, it has become imperative for many programs to use their review processes as a means to interpret, or perhaps offset, the perceived meaning of the rankings.

The following excerpt from an earlier work uses three program outcomes from an art and design undergraduate program:

1. Students will demonstrate the ability to critique orally and in writing other students' artifacts using appropriate art and design criteria.

2. Students will be able to respond to their peers' critique of their artifact by restating the main points of the criticism and either defending or responding with a solution of how to improve the artifact using appropriate Art and Design criteria.

3. Students will demonstrate their understanding of managing a studio by renting a studio through the University to Community Young Artists in Training Program.

Now, what do these outcomes have to do with graduation rates that are used in ranking comparisons? Through the articulation and assessment of outcomes such as these, a program can continue to monitor its acceptance rates, retention rates, and graduation rates; yet, it has more information to explain what is happening in the program to affect those rates and, thus, much more information about quality. For example, this program's ability to demonstrate that its students can apply, provide, and receive artistic critique of their work not only demonstrates that they are learning and are able to apply what is being taught in the classroom and the studio, but it also prepares them for the real experience of their profession. In addition, finding out that a student is unable to receive criticism about his or her work may mean that that student will leave this program—and, possibly, the university. Two likely directions for conversation among the faculty and program planners arise: (1) We need to evaluate more carefully how we provide feedback and criticism to our students, and/or (2) We need to have more information about recruiting practices to make sure that one of the criteria for admission to our program is evidence of the student's ability to take and use constructive feedback. In addition, evidence of students' abilities to accept criticism in their work and then apply that feedback to improve their work is evidence the program can use to recruit higher quality students and to entice potential employers of their students. In short, having this kind of information to improve programs and, thus, inform and possibly even influence persistence rates, graduation rates, and other measures is the first step toward usefulness. Then, program faculty and planners may adjust, if necessary, how this program recruits or operates—modifications that may constitute the second step toward meaningful and information-based program improvement. Clearly, this way of thinking and its natural movement toward subsequent procedures are much more valuable than just having enrollment management statistics that leave us to guess—sometimes rather wildly—about next steps.

Further examination of the student's ability to set up a small studio in the community through the university/community grant program ties the student to the university and the community itself. Not only is the student demonstrating what he/she has learned, the student may be increasing his/her engagement in the community and thus be more likely to stay in the area and contribute to the local economy. And if ongoing student/graduate contributions to the local economy are important, as they are with many small or regional institutions or with many highly specialized areas of study in particular, this kind of evidence is also critical evidence of impact and effectiveness. Again, this program is gathering rich information of how it may impact the performance indicators that its decision-makers truly value. (Bresciani and Allen, 2004, p. 1)

Another way to use national indicators is to direct program reviews to better understand what national rankings may mean for an institution. The following is an example from the University of Wisconsin-Whitewater, where results from the National Survey of Student Engagement (NSSE) directed creation of a special section in the institution's program review process. The University of Wisconsin, Whitewater's provost appointed a university-wide ad hoc committee to examine the results of the NSSE, in which the responses of UW-Whitewater (UW-W) students were compared to national norms. One of the areas in which the UW-W students' scores deviated from national figures was diversity awareness. That is, UW-W students reported that they were less likely to have conversations with persons from other races/ethnicities than their counterparts nationally. Among the committee's recommendations was "that all instructors review their curricula and other activities to identify and catalog where students are given opportunities to interact with people from diverse backgrounds" (UW-W NSSE Committee Report, Executive Summary). In addressing this issue, the Audit and Review Committee added a question to the self-study that requires all programs to specify how their programs address diversity and global awareness. Thus, when programs complete their self-studies for audit and review, an assessment of diversity awareness is an integral part of the process.

Finally, rankings such as those generated historically by the National Research Council for quality graduate programs may signal to institutions where they may need to increase their research and publication productivity to keep their programs competitive. Again, however, if programs also undergo graduate outcomes-based program review, they can discern through other means why their research and publication productivity is increasing or decreasing and whether that increase or decrease is desired and is part of their overall institutional or college plan.

Personnel Evaluations

Sixty-seven percent of the institutions reported that it is somewhat to very important for program review results to inform personnel evaluations. This is a challenging issue, and the implementation of this concept is not consistent. For example, some institutions, such as North Carolina State University, expect personnel to complete program reviews, so whether they comply with this requirement as a part of their job expectations may be, depending on their supervisor, a part of their individual performance review. However, in this scenario, the results of the program review are not used for personnel evaluations. The only criterion that is used is whether they have completed the evaluation. Program review results may be used, instead, to recommend professional development, but they may not be used to place a letter of reprimand in the faculty or staff member's personnel folder.

Here is an example of using program review results for professional development: A graduate faculty member at one good practice university is expected to teach and evaluate students' writing and speaking abilities in a course. After one year of teaching, she learned that her students were not improving their writing. After sharing these results with her department head, she was referred to an on-campus faculty development program from which she received a stipend to participate in a semester-long workshop, and she reworked her course syllabi to embed teaching and evaluation of students' writing into the course as she is teaching students and evaluating their learning about the course content. When she implemented this revised syllabus the following semester, the students' writing improved dramatically, thus improving the academic program outcomes for students' writing.

In this example, the course evaluation was not used to evaluate the faculty's teaching performance. However, she did feel that it was used to provide an opportunity for professional development so she could improve the intended outcomes she had articulated for her course and the writing outcomes that were articulated for the program.

The danger in using actual program review results in personnel evaluations, rather than using the information to determine whether the quality of the review process has improved, is that the quality review process may be compromised. Human beings are human beings, and there may be a tendency to share only the positive results of program review if faculty fear personal retribution for exposing something that may not be working as expected. In addition, many programs depend on other programs to help them meet their outcomes. Failure of one office to meet requirements that depend on another and holding those personnel accountable for the failure may lead to further work isolation.

The following example from one good practice institution illustrates how disconnects in administrative offices can be improved without using personnel evaluations. When the financial aid office set an outcome to award full financial aid packages to the highest academically prepared students by a specific date and learned that it was not accomplishing this outcome, the result could have been to reprimand the administrators in charge of this process. However, since the leadership was committed to evaluating the process, rather than the personnel, and since it had assessment methods in place to help identify the problems, the office learned specifically what had occurred. While the admissions office was growing increasingly frustrated with the financial aid office, assuming its top applicants were going elsewhere because the financial aid office staff could not get award letters out faster than the competition, the real culprit turned out to be an internal institutional information transfer process. The late award letters were due to the fact that colleges awarding merit scholarships had some overlap, and some were late in posting awards to the financial aid office, which caused the financial aid office to have to repackage awards after seeking clarification from the colleges. Furthermore, it was discovered that some colleges were competing with each other, awarding the same students different amounts of money in an attempt to recruit them. The solution was revising the process by which the colleges awarded and then notified the financial aid office of college-based awards, resulting in an increased number of on-time award letters to top students. This scenario further illustrates that when units participate in outcomes-based assessment program review to improve programs without adversely affecting personnel evaluations, these units can collaborate to improve more than one program's outcomes.

Inform Institutional Goals

One hundred percent of the institutions reported that it is somewhat to very important for programs to link their program outcomes to institutional goals. An example of this linkage comes from Keystone College:

Keystone College

Keystone College was founded as a private academy in 1868 and became an independent junior college in 1936. As the college expanded its four-year curricula from the original two programs to sixteen, the faculty and administration agreed that they had an extraordinary opportunity to examine what a baccalaureate education truly means. Committing to accountability and transparency was intrinsic to the evolution of the institution, with new programs having the opportunity to integrate goals, objectives, outcomes, and assessment from the outset and develop their ability to use these concepts as they grow.

Of major significance at Keystone is the fact that when the institution's evolution made it necessary to expand the college's general education requirements to a baccalaureate level, the faculty carefully articulated general education objectives that can be and are delivered through courses in the students' majors, thereby forging an important link between general education and specialization in the major. The following graphic explains how Keystone College works to integrate all of its academic offerings:

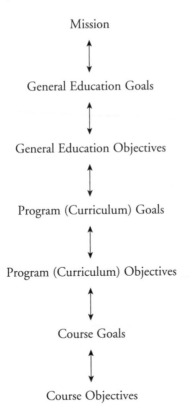

Mission

General Education Goals

General Education Objectives

Program (Curriculum) Goals

Program (Curriculum) Objectives

Course Goals

Course Objectives

This graphic shows an important aspect of all assessment and program review efforts at Keystone College: there is an inherent dialectic modality to the overall academic structure of the institution. Each level of the structure is informed and affected by the ones above and below. The mission of the college determines what majors and courses the college offers, and the specifics in any and all courses support the overall educational mission of the college.

Understanding the need for articulating goals, objectives, and outcomes, as well as determining methods for assessing the outcomes and reviewing the programs, is growing right along with the programs themselves as Keystone College continues its evolution into a full-fledged baccalaureate general college. (Submitted by Sherry Strain, Keystone College)

Linking program outcomes to institutional goals allows the institution to illustrate how it delivers its values and to evaluate how well the institution is achieving its mission. Having this kind of linkage obviously provides the institution with specific information about where and how to improve. It also allows the institution, as illustrated in the good practice institution mentioned above, to transform intentionally in accordance with its vision.

Inform Strategic Planning

One hundred percent of the institutions reported that it is somewhat to very important for program review results to inform institutional strategic planning. IUPUI, for example, has found in its several years of program review that it is imperative to link program review findings and processes to strategic planning. Furthermore, it has reported improvements in strategic planning, particularly for purposes of identifying program strengths, specific student outcomes, and future hiring priorities.

In addition to improvements in strategic planning, IUPUI reports that the program review process has generated a large list of recommendations for improvement that have been implemented in

- departmental advisory committees of community stakeholders;
- new, stronger alliances with business, industry, government, and philanthropic organizations;
- mentoring programs for junior faculty;
- revision of faculty workload standards and teaching assignments;
- updated curriculum plans;
- new methods for teaching large introductory classes;

- improved learning assessment techniques;
- reevaluation of course prerequisites; and
- changes in courses recommended to fulfill general education requirements. (Submitted by Trudy Banta and Karen Black, IUPUI)

Inform Budget Allocations and Reallocations

One hundred percent of the institutions reported that it is somewhat to very important for program review results to be used to inform program budget decisions within *departments*, and 67 percent reported the same level of importance for informing program budget decisions within *colleges*. For example, California State, Monterey Bay, asks faculty and staff in each program to reflect on operational efficiency by responding to the question, "Are full-time and part-time faculty engaged in levels of direct instruction which meet the expectations adopted in the planning and budgeting process?" (submitted by Richard Harris, Marsha Moroh, Joe Larkin, Octavio Villalpando, John Laughton, Judith White, Herb Martin, Suzanne Worcester, Josina Makau; California State, Monterey Bay; for more information on CSU-MB's process, see http://styluspub.com/resources/outcomes-basedprogram review.aspx).

At North Carolina State University, the use of compact planning asks that administrative and academic programs request funding for new initiatives by using outcomes-based assessment results to inform budgeting requests.

Whether an institution uses program review results to continue to improve its finest programs or it uses results to determine which programs should receive equity funding or funding to improve deficits, the point is that program review results can be used to allocate resources where there is evidence that they are needed. While no institution has enough money for all of its programs to become leaders in their own right, outcomes-based assessment program review can inform budget conversations and encourage tough prioritization that grows increasingly more necessary each day.

Institutional Shared Learning Principles

One hundred percent of the institutions reported that it is somewhat to very important for program review results to be used to inform conversations about institutionally shared competency expectations for student learning. Articulation of shared student learning principles, outcomes, goals, or competencies is growing increasingly more important as institutions explain their unique educational experience. The National Research Council, the American Association of Colleges and Universities, and the National Association of Student Personnel Administrators/American College Personnel Association, among many others, have called for institutions to clarify what they expect students to know and be able to do upon graduation regardless of their discipline.

Professional accreditors and associations of all types have designed standards and competencies they expect graduate and undergraduate students in particular disciplines to know and be able to demonstrate. Administrative and research units are also guided, in many instances, by professional standards and guidelines that demand that practitioners of certain professional administrative practices be able to demonstrate specific competencies as well. While in most cases for administrative practitioners, no accreditation is tied to their ability to demonstrate the competencies, the point illustrates that there are, indeed, quality controls for that profession.

Alverno College is a role model of how outcomes-based assessment program review informed an institution's shared student learning principles. IUPUI and Texas A&M also have shared student learning principles for undergraduate education that are evaluated through program review processes in the curriculum and co-curriculum. Isothermal Community College and the Maryland Community College Dean of Students formulated their student learning principles through planning for outcomes-based assessment. Furthermore, professional programs at California State University, Sacramento, and Truman State University used professional accreditation requirements to refer back to program outcomes and evaluation. As Truman State explains,

> Perhaps most importantly, faculty, through the process of assessment research, were prompted to reflect on program mission and goals and engage their colleagues in meaningful conversations about their expectations for teaching and learning. Ultimately, program faculty began to value assessment more and to become more involved in assessment in their disciplines. The essential engagement of faculty in assessment and in the process of program review has contributed to building and sustaining a culture of continuous quality improvement across the University. (Submitted by Truman State University)

The results are similar for good practice administrative programs. At Oregon State University, student affairs professionals demonstrate that they meet the Council of Standards guidelines for their programs (e.g., common standards of excellence) in addition to evaluating their programs' individual contributions to student learning and development.

Criterion 4: Awards and Recognition

Similar to the criterion of "Use of Results," this criterion has several subcategories. Illustrations of each subcategory follow.

Awards: Only 67 percent of the institutions reported that it is somewhat to very important for awards to be presented to programs in recognition of outstanding implementation of the program review process; only 60 percent thought it is somewhat to very important for awards to be presented to programs in recognition of outstanding contributions to *student learning* as discovered in the program review process.

Some of the good practice institutions have developed criteria for presenting specific awards for assessment to individual faculty and staff or to departments for having engaged in high-quality self-review processes. In some instances, monetary rewards or professional development opportunities accompany these awards. In other instances, the criteria for engaging in meaningful self-review of courses, projects, and programs are subset criteria for larger awards that recognize good teaching, research, and service. Such subset criteria allow the institution to illustrate that assessment does not exist for its own sake; rather, assessment is an embedded activity of quality teaching, research, and service.

In addition, some professional organizations present awards to programs that demonstrate through the use of outcomes-based assessment that their programs are good practices. Such awards reinforce that outcomes-based assessment can, indeed, improve programs and demonstrate their contributions to their intended outcomes.

Public Statements: One hundred percent of the institutions reported that it is somewhat to very important that administrators make public statements in support of the program review process. Many of the good practice institutions intentionally construct meaningful ways to provide opportunities for their senior-level administrators and respected faculty to highlight in public settings the importance and value of engaging in outcomes-based assessment program review. These speaking venues include faculty and staff orientation sessions; departmental, college/division, and university-wide councils and committees meetings; honors convocations; university-wide presidential addresses; commencement ceremonies; special retreats and planning sessions; and budget hearings.

Assessment Conferences, Symposia, Institutes, or Forums: Eighty percent of the institutions reported that it is somewhat to very important for *faculty* to have an opportunity to publicly and annually showcase their successful program review processes, while only 60 percent reported that it is somewhat to very important for *staff* to have an opportunity to publicly and annually showcase their successful program review processes. Only 53 percent of the institutions reported that it is somewhat to very important for individuals who complete successful program reviews to be expected to present their work publicly. In addition, 60 percent of the institutions reported that it is somewhat to very important for there to be at least one day annually where results of program review findings and how student learning and development have improved are shared throughout the campus community.

Many of the good practice institutions host a one- to three-day assessment conference where their own faculty and staff present assessment findings and lessons learned in regard to improving the evaluation process. In some cases, faculty and administrators from other institutions are invited to present or just attend. Good practice institutions report that these conferences provide an opportunity for their own faculty and staff to display good practices and to learn from other good practices. These venues also enable faculty and administrators to connect with one another and realize they are not the only ones struggling with similar questions and concerns. Evaluations of these learning opportunities conclude that faculty and administrative participants find encouragement to continue good practice work because they are inspired by conference participants' reactions to their work and are energized by finding others who care about quality in higher education.

Promotion and Tenure: Ninety-three percent of the institutions reported that it is somewhat to very important for engagement in program review to be viewed positively when faculty are considered for promotion and tenure. This conversation remains challenging for many research extensive institutions, which tend to promote and grant tenure to faculty primarily on the basis of research productivity. While many of these institutions encourage conversations around meaningful ways to promote and reward faculty for engagement in outcomes-based assessment, challenges remain. The option of addressing assessment as a legitimate research question with its own methodologies and methods, as well as publication venues, may begin to address these challenges. In addition, incorporating promotion and tenure processes that reward faculty for collaborative conversations about improving student learning may also prove to be beneficial. It is difficult to encourage faculty to commit time to the collaborative conversations needed to reform curricular and teaching strategies when promotion and tenure processes are often based on individual faculty achievements.

Institutions such as Alverno College are able to integrate engagement in outcomes-based assessment with the review of teaching. Outcomes-based assessment's embedded nature allows faculty to be considered for promotion based on the quality of their teaching and scholarship of assessment. Other institutions consider engagement in outcomes-based assessment as part of the service portfolio.

Administrative units across all types of institutions have more flexibility in promoting administrators based on their level of engagement in outcomes-based assessment. In addition, Oregon State University's Division of Student Affairs expects a commitment to outcomes-based assessment of all hires, as does North Carolina State University's Division of Undergraduate Affairs.

Criterion 5: Resources to Support Program Review

Budget: Ninety-three percent of the institutions reported that it is somewhat to very important for a *departmental budget* to be established for the program review process, 73 percent thought it is somewhat to very important for a *college/division budget* to be established for the program review process, and 87 percent felt the same about establishing an *institution budget.*

The variance in these responses may be due to institutional culture. In some institutions, it is customary for professionally accredited programs to drive the primary funding and support for institutional assessment. In other institutions, the budget is primarily centralized, and departments have smaller allocations for implementation or suballocations from the central budget. The most important take-away lesson from this section is that a budget for genuine engagement in outcomes-based assessment program review must be established. Whether it is established at the institutional or department level depends on the institutional culture. The institution may choose to centralize some facets of the operation and decentralize others, so budget allocations would follow suit.

In the establishment of an outcomes-based assessment program review budget, a system for reallocation or budgeting for recommended improvements revealed in the program review process is also important in improving programs and in validating the work of the outcomes-based assessment program review process. At John Carroll University, information garnered from program review is used to improve programs and services and to enhance the overall student learning process. For example, information from the division-wide College Student Survey (CSS) provided data regarding student perceptions about the limited sense of community on campus. Engagement in community is a core student learning principle for John Carroll, so improving the sense of community is a primary commitment. Consequently, the university reallocated funding to augment student programming and student government resources to enhance student life on campus. CSS results in subsequent years reflected an increase in satisfaction with student life and a greater sense of community on campus.

External Grants: Forty percent of the institutions reported that it is somewhat to very important to seek external grant funding for program review. Indiana University–Purdue University Indianapolis, for example, has been very successful in securing external grants to advance the work of its outcomes-based assessment program review process. Such grants have funded faculty and staff development initiatives as well as IUPUI's institution-wide electronic portfolio, which is accessible via its website.

Institutional Grants: Eighty-seven percent of the institutions reported that it is somewhat to very important for institutional grants to be used to fund outcomes-based assessment efforts. Truman State University has a long history and culture of assessment dating back to the early 1970s. A recent initiative, the establishment of campuswide Scholarship of Assessment Grants, seeks to improve the quality of student learning and development and to further enhance the culture of assessment on campus through faculty participation in assessment research. The summer grants are open to all full-time faculty and staff and may focus on either university-wide or discipline-level student learning outcomes.

Since the inception of these grants at Truman State in 2003, eleven projects have been funded, including four that focused specifically on discipline assessment. These projects were undertaken in the business and accountancy, biology, history, and communication disorders disciplines by discipline faculty. In every case, faculty used the grant funding either to initiate or to further develop assessment of student learning and development in their disciplines. Three projects have been completed and are summarized below.

Truman State University: Business and Accounting

In business and accountancy, faculty were interested in defining and assessing team skills for their majors, one of the key elements of the division's newly adopted mission statement. Working collaboratively with communication from faculty and the university's assessment specialist, the business and accountancy faculty incorporated input from faculty, students, and the current literature to develop a team skills assessment. Definitions and behaviorally anchored rubrics were designed to assess both individual team members and the team as a whole. The rubrics are now being used and refined in classrooms across the disciplines and have been shared with the entire university community at an assessment colloquium.

Truman State University: Biology

Biology faculty wanted to investigate whether existing assessment instruments were providing reliable and valid data for making decisions about their program curriculum. Faculty evaluated the reliability and validity of assessment data from the biology major field test (MFT) and the university-wide Liberal Arts and Sciences Portfolio Project, paying particular attention to the curricular validity of these two assessment instruments. As a result of this study, the biology discipline learned which assessment tools might need to be adjusted and how, and whether other tools might be needed to assess student outcomes in critical learning areas. It was recommended, for example, that biology faculty teaching core courses review the biology MFT to determine where the curriculum matches the test items and, perhaps, write additional items to test for analysis and higher-order thinking that would be scored locally.

Truman State University: Communications Disorders

Dissatisfied with their current assessments, consisting of either a comprehensive exam or a thesis, the faculty of the communications disorders graduate program wanted to explore other assessment options. Their goals were to develop an assessment package that was compatible with professional standards and their program mission, goals, and outcomes, and that would include existing and new assessment tools and procedures. The faculty successfully designed a new assessment package for their students that was strongly aligned with academic and clinical curricula, combined summative and formative assessment, and provided students with the opportunity to demonstrate knowledge through oral and written presentations. Currently, program faculty are discussing the new assessment tools and procedures and, once approved, the new assessment package will be implemented fully in fall 2005.

All too often, faculty are expected to do assessment work in their respective academic disciplines, but are given little in the way of rewards for that work. The Scholarship of Assessment Grants at Truman exemplify good practice in assessment and program review. Faculty received institutional support to research assessment tools and techniques and to choose, design, or refine assessments to best suit their programs and their students. As a result, they were able to improve their assessments, a critical component in ensuring change and improvement in their programs.

Perhaps most important, faculty, through the process of assessment research, were prompted to reflect on program mission and goals and engage their colleagues in meaningful conversations about their expectations for teaching and learning. Ultimately, program faculty began to value assessment more and to become more involved in assessment in their disciplines. The essential engagement of faculty in assessment and in the program review process has contributed to building and sustaining a university-wide culture of continuous quality improvement. For further information regarding Truman's Scholarship of Assessment Grants, go to http://assessment .truman.edu/grants/.

Institutional Data and Database: One hundred percent of the institutions reported that it is "somewhat important to very important" for faculty and administrators to know where to locate routinely collected institutional data (e.g., enrollment trends, course registration patterns, faculty workload) for use in program review. Sinclair Community College provides an Annual Data Set that includes enrollment by course, degree, and certificate; frequency of course offerings; diversity and gender profile of students; county of residence; cost per full-time-equivalent student (FTE), cost per student, and contribution margin analysis; average class size; scheduling of sections by term and delivery mode and exceptions to the planning schedule; curriculum, including new courses, course revisions, new programs, program revisions, articulation agreements, and student outcomes (direct and indirect); and faculty ratio (full- and part-time), FTEs per faculty member, and reassigned time per faculty member. All data are provided with a five-year trend analysis.

Providing this type of easily accessible data by program allows program faculty and administrators to allocate more time to articulating and refining outcomes and refining the evaluation processes that provide them with richer data about how well their programs are accomplishing what they are intended.

Ninety-three percent of the institutions reported that it is somewhat to very important that there is an *institutional database* where annual and biannual assessment plans and results are posted. Eighty-seven percent of the institutions reported that it is somewhat to very important for there to be *systematic centralized use of documentation tools.* Truman State University keeps all of its institutional assessment plans and reports in a central location, as do many other good practice institutions. However, the extent to which these plans and portfolios are kept in a database varies, as does the sophistication of each database. Some good practice institutions use commercial products, and others have developed their own.

In all cases, it is important to each good practice institution to have flexibility in the centralized documentation tool so that each program can document in the most meaningful manner what is important to that program. Centralized documentation tools do make it easier for the university to address how it is improving student leaning and development, research, and service across division and college lines. While this conversation can occur without centralized documentation processes, doing so requires concentrated collaboration and more intense effort by those mining and evaluating the plans and reports.

Institutional Website: Eighty-seven percent of the institutions reported that it is somewhat to very important that there is an institutional website, where annual and biannual program assessment plans and results are posted. California State University, Sacramento, asks each program to turn in its program review on a CD to be placed in an institutional electronic portfolio. As mentioned earlier, IUPUI has an institutional portfolio that resides on its website, and Alverno College has programmatic portfolios available to those who have passwords for access.

The transparency of these websites can vary. As we mentioned earlier, individual institutions must address transparency in sharing data. However, assessment plans and reports can be posted to websites that require password protection. While no Web security system is foolproof, such precautions limit the transparency of the plans and reports if an institution wishes to do so.

Evaluation Tools: Sixty-seven percent of the institutions reported that it is somewhat to very important that all programs use a common set of evaluation tools to evaluate specific student learning outcomes. Common evaluation tools are typically more prevalent in the assessment of general education outcomes. When evaluating academic or administrative outcomes, each discipline and department tends to prefer its own faculty- or administrator-developed evaluation tools, which may not transfer across discipline and departmental lines. However, higher-level or cross-campus instruments administered centrally, such as the NSSE, may provide important indicators that allow programs to focus on assessing specific concerns.

Some good practice programs, such as Truman State University's, offer several common evaluation tools, while Alverno College's faculty works on developing shared rubrics for evaluating writing and speaking. Each system offers varying advantages to the program implementing it, and some faculty and staff appreciate the time-saving measures of shared evaluation tools. However, the burden still rests on those using these shared instruments to ensure a connection between the evaluation tool and the outcome being measured and the method by which the outcome is being delivered.

Given that, some good practice institutions prefer authentically developed instruments and are not concerned with comparable evaluation of learning principles across the institution let alone from one institution to another. While comparability of student learning data remains a controversial topic in the United States, keep in mind that if the purpose of outcomes-based assessment program review is for the individual program to determine its effectiveness, and to do so in an environment that is committed to objectivity and ethics, then improvement will occur. Determining whether the level of improvement or performance is good enough must start with each program's own faculty and staff. It can continue with invitations to review the program via external departmental and institutional peer review processes. This allows for responsible comparability versus comparability occurring without the proper context.

Faculty and Staff Development: Faculty and staff development was reported to be a major criterion for ensuring successful implementation of a systematic genuine process of purposeful reflection and planning. One hundred percent of the institutions reported that it is somewhat to very important that faculty development workshops are provided annually so *faculty* can learn how to do assessment; yet, only 87 percent of the institutions reported that it is somewhat to very important that staff development workshops are provided annually so *administrators* can learn how to do assessment. Eighty-seven percent of the institutions reported that it is somewhat to very important that *faculty development* for assessment be centrally funded but departmentally delivered; yet, 67 percent of the institutions reported that it is somewhat to very important for *administrator development* for assessment to be centrally funded but departmentally delivered. Eighty percent of the institutions reported that it is somewhat to very important for workshops to be held to help key decision makers understand and use the program review findings effectively.

Variances in perception of what should be funded centrally are a direct result of institutional culture. For the reasons stated earlier, it is imperative that you pay attention to institutional preferences for centralization of resources versus decentralization of resources. There are always opportunities to leverage expertise, but if a department will only value instruction from one of its own, then the university must pay attention to that reality.

One hundred percent of the institutions reported that it is somewhat to very important for there to be centralized, no-cost resources to assist faculty and staff in learning how to engage in effective program review processes. At John Carroll University, the Office of the Vice President for Student Affairs strives to improve the overall understanding of assessment by providing, at no cost to users, workshops and one-on-one training to directors and other members of the division. National experts share their knowledge of assessment with members of the Division of Student Affairs through half- and full-day workshops, and the assistant to the vice president for student affairs and members of the Student Affairs Assessment Team work with each director to improve department assessment plans and methods. In addition, the Office of the Assistant to the Vice President for Student Affairs frequently shares resources about assessment, which include literature specific to individual departments and actual assessment tools. Education and training about assessment is ongoing and has resulted in improved assessment efforts in the Division of Student Affairs.

Depending on the good practice institution's perspective, faculty and staff development programs are intertwined with the outcomes-based assessment process itself, as it is at Alverno College, Isothermal Community College, and the Maryland Community Colleges. Others, such as Truman State University, North Carolina State University, and California State, Monterey Bay, offer comprehensive faculty and staff development programs in varying venues across the institution. IUPUI provides its university community with an annual professional Assessment Institute during which international experts engage with university practitioners and experts in a mutually beneficial learning environment.

Ninety-three percent of the institutions reported that it is somewhat to very important that presentations about how to do program review are designed for co-curricular departments to best meet the staff's learning needs and be specially designed for academic departments to best meet the faculty's learning needs. Oregon State and Texas A&M universities have ongoing staff development workshops for their co-curricular specialists. The institution-wide assessment symposium at Oregon State University began as a means for student affairs professionals to demonstrate what they learned through outcomes-based assessment and provide additional learning to those engaged in such assessment. Faculty and other administrative units are invited to Oregon State's annual symposium, which has resulted in a university-wide assessment committee that has begun to focus on institution-wide student learning principles. Student affairs representatives from Maryland Community Colleges meet twice a year for shared professional development opportunities, which has resulted in the articulation of shared learning outcomes.

Criterion 6: Coordination of the Process

Each good practice institution has varying models for coordinating the process. Eighty percent of the institutions reported that it is somewhat to very important for one institutional office or full-time person to coordinate the program review process for the entire university, but for program review to be delivered by units with supervisory authority of the programs being reviewed. Coordination of the university process, similar to other aspects we address in this book, is an evolutionary process. At some points in the organization and delivery of good practice outcomes-based program review, it may be wise for institutions to have centralized processes in the beginning and then decentralize the process as units learn about outcomes-based assessment and how to implement it in their day-to-day work.

In other cases, good practice may emerge from a decentralized good practice of one unit and spread to other units in the organization. As the decentralized process begins to spread, it may be helpful to have some centralized coordination of the various processes emerge so the university can report comprehensively on how the outcomes-based assessment program review process has improved institutional values.

In either model, it is important, as has been emphasized, to pay particular attention to institutional culture so that there is continuous balance in administrative requirements and faculty- and staff-driven assessment of values. This balance will be evident in the chosen institutional model for coordinating outcomes-based program review.

Criterion 7: Flexibility

One hundred percent of the institutions reported that it is somewhat to very important to have flexibility in implementing the program review process, so that each program can maintain its autonomy and manage its own resources and demands. As one can see from the good practice institutions' responses, providing those resources may be the most valuable aspect to implement. While it appears at first that it may be inexpensive for the institution to provide flexibility to programs for their administrative and academic outcomes-based assessment, the cost of this flexibility usually is incurred at the centralized location where program review coordination occurs.

For example, it is much easier to manage outcomes-based assessment program review for universities and colleges when they have the same process, timeline, reporting requirements, staff development, and implementation procedures; yet, there is a loss of autonomy and, thus, of the necessary flexibility required for individual academic and administrative programs to succeed in this purposeful reflection process. Therefore, flexibility must be maintained, and the administrative cost of organizing such flexibility will most likely be absorbed at the central university level.

Criterion 8: Addressing Barriers

One hundred percent of the institutions reported that it is somewhat to very important to have a process for addressing barriers to implementing program review, regardless of whether these barriers are expressed by faculty or staff. The importance of overcoming barriers is very real. The reasons shared for not engaging in meaningful outcomes-based assessment are very real to the person providing them. Sometimes the "excuse" may be a convenient reason for not participating; however, if you listen to the one providing the reason, you can determine whether it is an attempt to get out of engaging in the process or a true barrier. Often, what faculty or staff report as a barrier is not the barrier at all. Through thorough questioning, you can discover the genuine concern.

Sometimes it is helpful to propose the following analogy, which may assist in drawing out the specific barrier or resources that faculty and staff feel they need before being able to engage in genuine outcomes-based program review:

> We understand that you all feel that you are treading water, trying to stay afloat amidst the ever-increasing storm. While we are trying to illustrate that we have a stroke that we can teach you that will get you out of the stormy waters or at least be able to feel that you are master of the water, you feel that if you stop treading, you may sink and drown or, at the very least, sink and take in some nasty-tasting water. So, our question is, what specific life jacket can we throw you so that you feel you have time to learn the stroke we want to teach you and over time, master the storm? (personal communication during a faculty department meeting, March 3, 2005)

Barriers are real and they can prevent an institution from implementing meaningful outcomes-based assessment; however, sincere and genuine attempts to address barriers will reap benefits. More information on barriers and strategies to address them is found in chapter 6.

Criterion 9: An Evaluation of the Program Review Process

One hundred percent of the institutions reported that it is somewhat to very important for a multiyear assessment plan to be in place to evaluate the effectiveness of outcomes-based assessment program review. Ninety-three percent of the institutions reported that it is somewhat to very important to have teams of *faculty* educated to review the quality of the program's individual review process, while 87 percent felt that it is somewhat to very important to have teams of *administrators* educated to review the quality of the program's individual review process. Eighty-seven percent of the institutions reported that it is somewhat to very important for *external consultants* to review the effectiveness of the program review process.

Each of the good practice programs has its own means to evaluate how effective it has been in implementing meaningful and manageable outcomes-based assessment program review. Many of the criteria used in those evaluative processes are contained in this chapter. Several resources can assist institutions in such evaluations, the most extensive of which may be the Levels of Implementation Rubrics provided by the Higher Learning Commission: http://www.ncahigherlearningcommission.org/resources/assessment/index .html. In addition, sample meta-assessment plans and rubrics can be found in appendix K. Most important is to identify how your institution will know that its efforts at outcomes-based assessment program review have been effective and have resulted in the improvements they were intended to make.

Conducting such a meta-assessment prevents the process from taking on a life of its own. Recall the purpose of outcomes-based assessment program review. Some who are engaged in it get so caught up in the "rules" or guidelines they forget that the process exists to assist in the systematic reflection of student learning and other administrative functions so that they can be improved.

Because implementation of a pervasive process takes time, those engaged in it may become discouraged if they do not step back, analyze the process itself, and see whence the institution has come. Short- and long-term goals, outcomes, evaluation methods, and results must be used to recognize accomplishments in the process. In addition, the same must be done to identify opportunities for improving the process itself. In so doing, those using the process are practicing what they preach and reaping the benefit of improvements in their own process, which, in turn, should improve the quality of higher education within their own institutions.

5

KEY QUESTIONS TO CONSIDER WHEN IMPLEMENTING GOOD PRACTICE OUTCOMES-BASED ASSESSMENT PROGRAM REVIEW

Having examined good practice templates and criteria for evaluation and being referred to good practice case studies in the appendices, you may now wonder how to start building your own good practice outcomes-based assessment program review. Like the previous chapters, this chapter is not prescriptive; it is intended to provide some basic steps and references for implementing outcomes-based assessment program review at any institution. However, as in the previous chapters, you should pay close attention to your own institutional culture when answering these questions.

The suggestions and questions posed in this chapter are drawn from the compilation of good practice institutions and are affirmed throughout a variety of sources of literature, such as Banta and Associates (2002); Bresciani at el. (2004); Huba and Freed (2000); Lee (2004); Maki (2004); Palomba and Banta (1999); and Suskie (2004). The questions posed in this chapter are for you to answer with your own program review faculty and staff. As you address certain questions, you will discover typical barriers to implementing outcomes-based assessment program review. Ideas and suggestions for addressing those barriers are presented, along with good practice examples for overcoming the barriers, in chapter 6.

Create a Well-Represented, Well-Respected Committee

As mentioned earlier, when planning program review, one of the first key steps is to bring together a group of committed and respected faculty and co-curricular professionals to plan the process. Bringing together well-represented and well-respected faculty and administrative professionals is instrumental to building a well-informed and meaningful process. In forming your group of faculty and co-curricular professionals, you may want to consider the following:

- Who cares enough about quality in research, teaching, service, and student learning to commit his or her time? Invite these professionals to the table.
- Who is well respected in their fields? Invite these professionals to the table.
- Do you have appropriate representation of all of the areas that should be represented?
- If you have unions, are they represented?
- Do you have advocates for improvement involved as well as those who have negative feelings about the process?

As you form your group, keep membership open, meeting notes public—yet carefully edited—and let anyone attend who wants to. If you have been meeting for a while and a new group of faculty or administrators wants to join, allow the group to join—making special time to meet with its members before their first meeting to update them on what has happened thus far. The time involved in updating new members allows them to contribute immediately; it also keeps the members who have been attending meetings for a while from feeling as if they are rehashing the same topics.

Meeting Times and Agendas

Setting meeting schedules (times, locations, and frequency) often involves intricate aspects of institutional culture. Pay attention to your institutional culture and do not move faster or slower than the norm. Doing so could cause many to question the motives behind and sustainability of what you are trying to accomplish. For example, some institutions think about preparing for their accreditation review late in the game, then must hurry to get organized. Such hurrying causes many to think that the only reason they are organizing is for the accreditation review, not because the institution is trying to prepare itself for meaningful, long-term self-reflection and improved decision making via evidence.

Furthermore, never call a meeting without first establishing an agenda. Stay organized, and if you don't have any business for the committee, task force, work group, or advisory committee (or whatever you choose to call it), cancel the meeting.

Questions to ask yourself include the following:

- How regularly do we want to meet?
- How long do we want to meet?
- When are the best days and times to meet? Should we vary meeting times and days to allow those whose teaching schedules conflict an opportunity to attend?
- Where should we meet?
- Do we need to set aside longer retreat or planning times? If so, how long should they be and how often? When and where would be the most relaxing environment for the committee to plan?
- Are we continually choosing a meeting time or location that appears to purposefully exclude one group or another from joining the conversations?

Keep in mind that when you are starting out, you may not know the answers to these questions, so be sure to allow yourself some flexibility in scheduling. Also, keep true to the practice of outcomes-based assessment and allow yourself to improve and refine your meeting schedule as your committee work evolves or as subcommittees become more active.

Organize the Committee's Role and Responsibilities

Similar to the previous points, it may be difficult at first to establish and maintain a committee's role, but be forthright with faculty and administrators and allow the committee to evolve as its thinking and work evolves. It is important to provide faculty and co-curricular professionals with some sort of direction about what the committee needs to accomplish before you invite them to join. Whether a formal charge is necessary again depends on institutional culture. Sinclair Community College provides its committees with

roles and functions and very specific assignments (see http://www
.sinclair.edu/about/assessment/index.cfm).

Questions to ask when creating the role of the committee include the
following:

- Will the members define what "outcomes-based assessment program
  review" means for the institution or college/division or other unit(s)?
- Will this committee draft the conceptual framework for outcomes-
  based assessment program review?
- Will this committee draft the common operational language for out-
  comes-based assessment program review?
- Will committee members draft the guidelines for outcomes-based as-
  sessment program review?
- Will members determine the assessment plan and assessment report
  templates?
- What will the committee's primary role be? Will it have any secondary
  role(s)?
  ○ Advisory?
  ○ Training/educating others?
  ○ Providing and administering assessment resources?
  ○ Evaluating the program review process?
  ○ Evaluating the program review content?
- Given the primary role, do you have the most appropriate representa-
  tion on the committee?
- Will this committee be the support system for the entire program re-
  view process, or will professional staff be involved?
- Is the committee permanently identified and appropriately recognized
  by the university?
- How will the work the committee generates be vetted by others in an
  appropriate and timely manner?
- How will the committee members educate themselves about out-
  comes-based assessment?
- How will they stay motivated to promote outcomes-based assessment?
- How and how often will new members be rotated onto the
  committee?
- Will the committee have permanent, or ongoing, faculty/co-curricular
  professional fellows as members?

- Will the committee be supported primarily by a vice president's office? By the president's office? By the provost? By whom?
- What responsibilities will be delegated to college/division or departmental committees and what responsibilities will remain with a university-level committee? For example, at the U.S. Naval Academy, the agencies responsible for assessment include the departments and centers responsible for student learning, the academic and professional development divisions responsible for the core program, and the Faculty Senate Assessment Committee (formerly the Assessment Task Force) that is charged with oversight and coordination of the assessment process.

Once the committee is established, you may want to consider keeping all of the committee's work on a public website or, at least, a site that is public to the university community. Again, this openness allows others to join in as the committee addresses issues that interest them, and it encourages dialogue around institutional excellence and accountability, furthering ownership of those conversations and resulting decisions. It is good to remember that committee members will be less frustrated if they clearly understand their roles. You also may need more than one committee for the process. For example, you may want an overarching university committee to advise on the overall process of how outcomes-based assessment program review should work, but delegate review of the quality of the process to another committee or to each college/division.

Similarly important, if you are reading this book because you are charged with leading the outcomes-based assessment program review effort on your campus or within your college/division or department, you will be less frustrated if you articulate your own role or if you are assigned the task by the proper authority figure.

Questions for you and others to answer may include the following:

- Are you a facilitator of the process, or are you directing the process?
- Will you be an educator of the process, or will you do the work for the faculty and administrators?
- Will you investigate good practices and propose them to the committee? Who will determine the best way to adapt and apply good practices, or will the committee investigate good practices?

- Will you collect all of the program review documents in one central location, or will you know whom to contact within each program when it comes time to compile such documents?
- Will you write reports, or will you edit what the committee writes?
- Will you design the faculty and staff development components, or will you make recommendations for their design?
- Will you draft the meta-assessment (assessment plan) for outcomes-based assessment program review, or will you edit what the committee drafts?
- Will you conduct or coordinate the meta-assessment?
- Will you arrange for professional development of committee members, or will you coordinate their professional development through their representing departments/programs?
- Will you offer to educate college and division assessment committees, or will you just provide the educational resources?
- Will you assist in the creation of college/division committees, or will you just provide templates for their creation?
- How often will you ask college/division committees to monitor their own work and report on it so that you can ensure a quality and ethical review process across the campus?

Answering these questions and others will help inform everyone about what they should expect and from whom. Your answers should also organize the process in the beginning. As with most other processes, what you design in the beginning will evolve and take shape as your process does, so things will change. Flexibility is key to ensuring the autonomy needed for individual disciplines to explore and improve their own processes. Provide that flexibility within a framework of structure and be sure to update communication flow and documents to illustrate those changes.

Finally, make sure that everyone's role in the program review process is clear. Delineate who is involved in reviewing quality of the self-reflection process and who is responsible for reviewing quality of content. In regard to the latter, remember that the most effective improvements will be made if the review process of content is done first at a level close to where content is being delivered.

Articulate Expectations for Outcomes-Based Assessment Program Review

At an appropriate time, key leadership will need to inform the university community of the expectations for engaging in outcomes-based assessment program review. As discussed in the section regarding defining assessment and revisited in the short- and long-range goals section, an institution cannot ignore the political prowess of those demanding accountability and how those demands may play into faculty and staff's interpretations of what "really" is being requested and how it will be used. Therefore, it is imperative that at some point, the institution's or division/college's leadership articulate exactly what is expected from the outcomes-based assessment program review process.

Determining the appropriate time to announce the expectations for outcomes-based assessment program review may be challenging. It depends on the support process you have in place or the one you are planning to put in place. We all have our war stories about being asked to do something we have no clue how to do. Thus, before the key administrators announce expectations, it would be helpful to have educational support systems in place and examples of what you want to see occur. Doing so reduces panic among the faculty and administrators whose responsibility it will be to implement such a practice.

In some instances, the answers to some of these questions may vary by department or even program, depending on how much flexibility each department or program has.

- Why are we engaging in outcomes-based assessment program review?
- What value does it have for me as a faculty member/administrator?
- How will it make me a better faculty member/administrator?
- How will it improve my program?
- How will it affect my students?
- Is this institution required to do it? Why or why not?
- What is required for me to demonstrate my program's accomplishments?
- How often is a report needed?
- What is the review process for my report?
- Where do I find the time to do this?

- Where do I find the resources?
- Where do I learn how to do this?
- What assistance will I receive in completing the report?
- How will the results of my program review be used?
- Will one committee evaluate my program review for quality of the evaluation process?
- Will that same or another committee evaluate my program review for quality of content?
- Are external reviewers needed? Who pays for them?
- Who will see my report?
- How public will the review of my report be?
- Will the program review results be used to evaluate me personally?
- Will program/department/college/division/institutional reallocations be based on my program review findings?
- Will I receive an allocation to improve my program if the data demonstrate that funding is necessary?
- What happens if data reveal that someone else's program needs to be improved first in order for my program to be improved (e.g., poor performance in math competencies are affecting my student statisticians' learning)?
- Is there a university/division assessment plan timeline for implementation of this process?
- Will someone do the "regular" data collection (e.g., enrollment figures, retention and graduation rates, budget figures)? Who?
- Will someone coordinate the assessment planning process? Who?
- Will assessment plans be public? Will they be centrally located?
- Will someone be in charge of documentation? Who?
- How will program review results inform enrollment planning, performance indicators, and other types of evaluation?
- Can key assessment coordinators get release time or a stipend to establish the process?
- How will the institution manage the sometimes competing information requests from external and internal constituents?
- What will the rewards be for engaging in assessment?
- How will all of the university's planning and evaluation initiatives link?

- Are there institutional learning outcomes that all programs need to assess?
- What if programs and courses cannot link their outcomes to specific institutional goals?
- What happens if I don't engage in outcomes-based assessment program review?

These are just some of the questions that will need to be answered about the overall review process for each program. Again, these answers may come from institutional or college/division leadership, or they may come from a faculty committee or a faculty and co-curricular professional task force that proposes recommendations to institutional leadership for implementation, as was demonstrated at North Carolina State University (see the FAQ at http://www.ncsu.edu/undergrad_affairs/assessment/assess.htm). In some cases the answers may come individually from colleges and departments if their needs differ from each others'. It all depends on your institutional culture.

In time, these questions may subside as people see for themselves how much or how little program review is validated. Some of the good practice institutions no longer need to answer these questions, as they have demonstrated over several years how program review results have been used to improve programs. In the beginning, however, it is important to be consistent and to demonstrate (commitment of resources, public support for assessment, etc.) that the answers are true. Answering these questions in a public manner also allows the answers to serve as somewhat of an honor code as administrators and faculty members reach agreement and publish those agreements in the form of an online FAQ. The publicly published FAQs can serve as an honor code of practice and thus alleviate much of the anxiety of those engaged in outcomes-based assessment program review as they see some of their concerns worked out in a collegial manner.

When you are also new in implementing genuine institution-wide, outcomes-based assessment program review, you may not have the answers to all of these questions. That is normal. The authors encourage you to be forthright and allow your faculty/co-curricular committee to respond to those who are asking questions. You may get some fabulous ideas about how to answer these questions from those who are the most vocal.

Plan Short-, Mid-, and Long-Range Goals

When implementing or refining your institutional outcomes-based assessment program review process, you can quickly become discouraged if you intend to attain the good practices in this book in your first year. While you may be able to achieve many good practices quickly, you want to do so in a manner that allows for the practices to become second nature. As Alverno College illustrates in appendix K, some of their good practices are no longer required; they are, rather, part of the day-to-day routine. In other words, faculty and co-curricular professionals engage in these good practices as a part of their daily work, and, therefore, evidence of that practice appears without its even being requested. While that is what most institutions aspire to achieve, getting there takes time and consistent reinforcement of the value of self-reflection. Thus, planning your implementation strategies and evaluating how well you are transforming institutional decision-making culture may be best achieved with a series of short- and long-term goals.

Decide what you can accomplish in the short term. For example, some short-term goals may be to

- form the faculty/co-curricular committee that will guide the process;
- define outcomes-based assessment program review;
- draft the shared conceptual framework;
- draft the common operational language;
- draft the guidelines or template for assessment-based program review;
- identify which faculty and staff have already engaged in outcomes-based assessment program review and create a plan to leverage their expertise;
- identify resources that are already in place that can inform program improvement conversations;
- identify resources that are needed to embed evidence-based decision making in day-to-day work;
- deliver introductory workshops on how to engage in meaningful outcomes-based assessment program review; and
- embed explanations of program review expectations in orientation programs for faculty, staff, and students.

Long-range goals may be those goals that

- define what successful institutionalized outcomes-based assessment program review would look like;
- define which good practice criteria your institution will use to evaluate how well it has transformed into using evidence-based decision making to improve programs and articulate what it will look like when your institution meets those good practice criteria;
- define when programs have been improved because of the pervasive and systematic practice of outcomes-based assessment program review;
- define a learning-centered institution in all aspects of your institutional values;
- plan a comprehensive faculty and staff development program that includes new faculty and staff orientation and teacher assistant training programs; and
- draft a strategic plan for centrally and programmatically supporting the efforts of purposefully reflective practices for improving student learning, research, and service.

Working backward from your long-range goals, you can establish several other short- or mid-range goals, such as those that will lead to your achieving good practices in outcomes-based assessment program review. For example, one short- or mid-range goal may be to "deliver introductory workshops on how to engage in meaningful outcomes-based assessment program review." A next short- or mid-range goal that brings you closer to a long-range goal for a comprehensive faculty and staff development program may be that, two years after starting your introductory workshops, you have a series of specific workshops on methodologies and instruments to evaluate student learning. Two years later, you may add workshops for preparing reports that inform various constituents about what you are learning about student learning. Two years later, you may remove your introductory workshops in exchange for a new faculty and staff orientation program in each department.

The time frame for achieving good practices varies among types of institution. It varies even further based on key leadership commitment to evidence-based decision making or outcomes-based assessment program review. Most time frames for short- and long-range goals have to be adjusted due to the real-life influences that affect the work of those involved in institutionalizing outcomes-based assessment program review. Influences such as key leadership changes, governing board member changes, budget crises, institutional or government policy changes, and other reactions to political or media-driven demands can cause leadership to alter its focus from the pursuit of excellence to survival. While this shift is normal, the degree to which an institution allows normal higher education crises to hinder its ability to define who it is, and evaluate itself according to the stakeholders who deliver and receive the learning, will define the degree to which the institution refrains from progressing with its data-driven decision-making model.

While most faculty and staff involved in day-to-day implementation of outcomes-based assessment program review have little to no control over these higher education crises, they do have control over what the implementation plan looks like. For example, if an institution has established its short-, mid-, and long-range goals for implementing outcomes-based assessment program review, and it has a plan to evaluate the extent to which those goals are being achieved, then at least faculty and staff can draw to the attention of the leadership where the plan has deviated from the timeline. If a meta-assessment plan is being implemented, then faculty and staff can also illustrate what may be needed for the institution to move ahead in its purposeful self-reflection process. In this manner, the institution is "practicing what it preaches" in that it is evaluating its own achievement of meaningful, systematic, outcomes-based assessment program review. (See http://assessment.tamu.edu/StrategicPlanningforEBDM.html for a draft strategic plan for implementing outcomes-based assessment program review.)

When planning your short-, mid-, and long-range goals, consider the following questions:

- Who will define what outcomes-based assessment program review means for the institution or college/division? And when?
- Who will identify the political (or other) motivations for engaging in outcomes-based assessment program review (if any)? And when?
- Who will draft the conceptual framework for outcomes-based assessment program review? And when?
- Who will draft the common operational language for outcomes-based assessment program review? And when?
- Who will draft the guidelines for outcomes-based assessment program review? And when?

- Who will determine the assessment plan and assessment report templates? And when?
- Once these drafts and templates are completed, to whom do they go for review? For approval? For implementation? For funding?

Additional questions to consider are posed throughout the rest of this chapter.

Identify Existing Resources and Processes and New Resources

When starting anew with outcomes-based assessment program review, it is extremely helpful to identify what your institution has already done in regard to evaluation, assessment, or planning. In doing so, you often identify those who have already engaged in the process and can serve as your test case examples of success (Maki, 2004). (Keep in mind that because there may not be a standard definition for "assessment," one person may call outcomes-based assessment "planning," while another calls it "evaluation." Therefore, it is important not to limit your request based on how some people may interpret the definition.) In addition, these faculty and staff who are already engaged in outcomes-based assessment can assist in educating others, if they so choose, in how to engage in meaningful outcomes-based assessment program review. It also helps you identify colleagues who have already carved out a language. Inviting these faculty and staff to drafting the common operational language will ensure that those who are already doing assessment feel ownership in the refinement of the assessment process.

Beyond identifying faculty and staff who are already engaged in outcomes-based assessment and leveraging their expertise, you also learn about the processes in which they are involved and the resources they are already using. This exploration is a great way to identify who knows what and who is getting data from where. Such information can assist others in their quest for evidence of how well their program is accomplishing what they say it is.

When many programs are beginning their self-evaluations, it is particularly valuable to them to know where they can access data that most institutions have readily available. Yet, many institutions have not had the time or structure to organize data and make it easily accessible to faculty and staff. As the good practice institutions reported earlier, it is important that data be identified and made readily available. Then faculty and staff can spend more time exploring questions and searching for evidence of student learning that has not traditionally been so readily available.

Often, when administrators try to find out who is already engaged in these processes, they send out a survey. That may be helpful and productive, but it may be just as helpful to inquire informally about who is doing assessment and ask them to submit plans and reports of what they are learning from their assessment work. Doing this provides you with plenty of information about how they are conceptualizing outcomes-based assessment and with an idea of the language they are using as well as what they are learning about their program. It also means that they do not have to take time to complete another report or survey—rather, they can just turn in what they have been working on for the last few months or years. While it takes more of your time to compile such information, you have already begun to collect artifacts that demonstrate which programs are or are not engaged in meaningful reflection, and you have examples of how results are being used to improve student learning and development, research, and service.

Gathering these artifacts can also help you identify the types of outcomes that faculty and staff value. Identifying shared outcomes can lead to discussions about shared institutional learning principles. In addition, identifying the methods faculty and staff use to evaluate outcomes can assist you in identifying internal experts in the design of rubrics or portfolios, whose work you may ask permission to offer as examples to others who aspire to use those same methods.

Questions to ask include the following:

- Who is engaged in assessment/planning/evaluation/program review/ accreditation/institutional effectiveness/quality assurance/quality enhancement/evidence-based decision making/continuous improvement in their programs at your institution?
- What has the institution already done with the evaluation of general education/your academic program/your co-curricular program/your course/your activity?
- What data can you get from your state system office/state coordinating board/Institutional Research Office/Registrar's Office/Enrollment Services or Management Office/information system/Budget or Finance Office/Research Office/Public Relations Office/Strategic Planning Office?

- What national surveys (e.g., National Survey of Student Engagement [NSSE], Cooperative Institutional Research Program [CIRP], Your First College Year [YFCY], etc.) have already been completed, and where are the data located?
- What resources are already available to assist with this process (data, assessment tools, people, technology, workshops, tutorials, reference books, statisticians, psychologists, sociologists, educators, consultants, etc.)?

Once you have identified existing resources, you can move on to identifying the resources you may need to implement systematic and pervasive outcomes-based assessment program review. Keep in mind that most of the resources many of the good practice institutions enjoy now were not present when they first began their processes. So it may be wise to incorporate the acquisition of resources to support outcomes-based assessment program review into your strategic plan. By planning which resources you will need to support ongoing outcomes-based assessment program review, you will also be able to identify opportunities to reallocate resources within program review. For example, as faculty and administrators learn more about outcomes-based assessment, you may be able to reallocate centralized training materials into stipends for decentralized "faculty fellows." The faculty fellows, representing each college/division, can coordinate creation of educational materials, post them on the Web, and offer workshops as well as one-on-one consultation services to their own college/divisions. Furthermore, using faculty fellows allows materials to be customized for specific college/division needs, such as meeting professional accreditation requirements or specific college/division goals for learning or development, research, or service.

Some sample questions to ask when determining what new resources may be needed include the following:

1. Do you have adequate reference materials on outcomes-based assessment?
2. Do you need to organize data from your information systems into a Web-query database so faculty and administrators can access data they need for program review from their desktop?
3. Do you need templates created for departmental program review websites?

4. Do you need scanning software?
5. Do you need survey software?
6. Do you have a centralized place to store electronic or hard copies of program review plans and reports?
7. Do you need to hire a Web master to organize your program review plans and results on the Web?
8. Do you need tools to assist faculty with text mining?
9. Do you need funds to finance retreats where faculty can discuss improvements that have been informed by their program review efforts?
10. Do you need institutional grants to award release time to faculty and administrators who are designing rubrics and portfolios?
11. Do you need institutional grants to fund programs for proposed improvements?
12. Do you need institutional grants to send faculty and administrators to assessment conferences where they can learn about new practices while showcasing their own work?
13. Do you need more faculty and administrators to help with one-on-one consulting in regard to questions raised about outcomes-based assessment?
14. Do you need to hire statisticians to assist with data analysis?
15. Do you need to contract outside readers to review portfolios? Do you need funds to pay them?
16. Do you need to hire administrative assistants to assist with documentation?
17. Do you need to hire research assistants to conduct the meta-assessment?
18. Do you need to provide higher-level administrators with leave time so they can learn how to responsibly use the data generated from program review?

While this list of questions is not exhaustive, please note that it also does not mean that your institution needs to invest in all of this internal support for program review to become sustainable. Again, each institution is unique in its culture and, therefore, unique in how it adapts outcomes-based assessment program review. This list will help you think about what you may need as an institution to engage in this meaningful, evidence-based decision-making process.

In essence, what you are trying to accomplish by answering these questions is to determine the extent to which your institution is designing a support system for building and sustaining outcomes-based assessment program review. So it may also be extremely beneficial to pose the good practice criteria as questions to determine what resources you already have in place to demonstrate good practices.

Establish a Communication Plan

Chapter 2 highlighted the importance of communicating the value of outcomes-based assessment program review to administrators. The importance of doing so was emphasized further in chapter 3. However, how you go about communicating the value and importance of this evidence-based decision-making process depends, once again, on your institutional culture.

The following questions may help you discern the most productive means by which to communicate with all stakeholders:

1. Who will articulate assessment expectations?
2. How will those expectations be communicated?
3. How will the university community be informed about the plan?
4. How will the university community be informed about the resources that are available?
5. Will the university community have an opportunity to comment?
6. Does each college/division/department/program have its own unique communication structure? If so, how can you ensure that the structure is tapped to provide faculty with program review information and to bring important feedback to the program review committee?
7. Is it possible to have program review committee (the committee charged with reviewing the quality of process) representation from each college/division or department/program so the representative can serve as a conduit for information dissemination to and from the committee and to and from the program/department/college/division that he or she represents?

8. Will faculty and administrators check a program review website for updated information, or is it best to get that information out in a newsletter format, on a listserv, in a memorandum, or via all of these routes?

9. Which university/college standing committees should be informed of program review updates and how often?

10. Can program review committee members present evidence of what the institution is learning about program quality to departments at faculty or staff meetings?

11. Is it appropriate to use the campus media to "advertise" what faculty are learning about the quality of their programs?

12. Can the university public relations team help to communicate within the university and to external stakeholders what the university is learning about program quality?

13. Can the university or college enrollment management professionals use what the university is learning about program quality in their student recruitment materials?

14. Can program quality information be used to recruit and retain faculty and co-curricular professionals?

15. Is it appropriate to create a packet of materials about the university outcomes-based assessment program review process for faculty and administrators to use when applying for grants?

Discuss Implementation Barriers and Strategies to Overcome Them

Barriers are barriers, whether they are real or perceived. Chapter 6 addresses typical barriers and good practice strategies to overcome them.

Move Forward with Flexibility

As discussed in chapter 6, fear is one of the primary barriers to faculty and administrative involvement in outcomes-based assessment program review. Often, the only way to combat irrational fear is to engage in the activity you fear. Rock climbers who learn to climb to overcome their fear of height do indeed overcome the irrational fear by learning how to scale mountains safely. By using equipment that was designed for the task, by learning and practicing the skills, their confidence grows, and their irrational fear is replaced with a healthy respect for what they are undertaking and accomplishing. The same is true for scuba divers. The diver overcomes irrational fear of water by learning to trust in the equipment and his or her diving buddy. However, in both cases, the diver and the climber would have never been able to test their trust in their equipment and their climbing partner or dive buddy if they never even tried to climb or dive. No first climb is ever perfect, and no first scuba diving attempt is challenge-free.

The same is true for engaging in outcomes-based assessment program review. Faculty and staff need to learn how to do it, learn about the appropriate tools and resources to aid them, and learn to trust other faculty and administrators to use the data appropriately. In this manner, over time, faculty and staff can improve their own program review processes, just as the climber and the scuba diver improve. While divers have buddies who may disappoint them, faculty may be frustrated by their colleagues, yet the decision not to engage in a collaborative manner typically means you cannot improve the program. Responsible divers and rock climbers do not go it alone, even though they may be wary of their buddy or partner. Therefore, after faculty and staff learn how to engage in outcomes-based assessment, their next step is literally to dive in and implement it.

Keep in mind that if climbing and diving equipment go unchecked, the safety of the climber and the diver is at risk. Similarly, if faculty and staff jump in and do not check on the quality of their review processes, they may realize the very fears that originally kept them from becoming engaged, such as poor process and inappropriate methods, result in "bad" data and poor decision making. Therefore, continued improvement in the program review process should be monitored but done in a completely flexible manner.

While we have presented several tips and advice on implementing good practices in outcomes-based assessment program review, our most important advice is to remain flexible. The best of good practices can go awry if they are implemented with too much rigor and without regard for program autonomy.

In addition, it is wise to leverage faculty's and administrators' innate intellectual curiosity. The majority of higher education professionals do want to understand how to improve their programs, research, service, and student learning, and they want to use their own discipline-specific inquiry methods to do so. Leverage that knowledge and energy, and you will find that many implementation barriers will fade.

If you take away one piece of information from this book, let it be "to remain flexible in the implementation process." Pay close attention to how varying disciplines may need different schedules, report formats, or other elements of the process. Keep in mind that the ultimate goal is to engage faculty and staff in purposeful reflection, planning, and evaluation to improve their programs, research, service, and student learning.

A list of helpful implementation reminders follows:

1. Be flexible.
2. Define outcomes-based assessment program review and determine why your institution is engaging in it.
3. Articulate a shared conceptual framework for outcomes-based assessment program review.
4. Articulate a common operational language for outcomes-based assessment program review.
5. Clearly communicate expectations for engaging in outcomes-based assessment program review.
6. Clearly define how the results will be used.
7. Go ahead and write down every program outcome, but do not try to assess every program outcome every year (Bresciani et al., 2004).
   a. You may want to start with course outcomes and build program outcomes from those.
   b. You can start with institutional, college/division, or departmental goals and ask each program or course to align its outcomes to those goals.
   c. Then, move on to implementing the entire assessment cycle one outcome at a time making everything systematic; in other words, work on forming "habits" of assessment.
8. Be sure that faculty/administrators understand the purpose of assessment; it is not assessment for assessment's sake. Its goal is to reflect on the end result of doing so that the doing can be incorporated.
9. Be sure that faculty/administrators value what is being measured.
10. Be sure that faculty/administrators have ownership of the process.
11. Respect varying disciplines' academic autonomy.

12. Recruit respected and influential faculty/administrators to lead the process.
13. Remind each other of the benefits of assessment.
14. Share with each other examples of what works well and incorporate this into professional development opportunities and orientation programs.
15. Celebrate what you are learning about program quality through program review.
16. Advertise what you have learned about assessment and the decisions you have made.
17. Gently challenge faculty and staff to establish another good practice once they have mastered one good practice.
18. Incorporate students in all facets of assessment planning and implementation, if your program is ready and your institutional culture allows.
19. Acknowledge and address barriers to assessment.
20. Pay attention to varying program demands and resources.
21. Understand your role as a program review committee member.
22. Understand your role as the program review committee chair or professional responsible for the process.
23. Have the president and other appropriate institutional leaders show their gratitude to program review participants in a meaningful way.
24. Tie reallocation of resources to decisions and recommendations to improve student learning and development that are based on assessment results, if appropriate for your institution.
25. Be flexible.

6

OVERCOMING BARRIERS TO IMPLEMENTING OUTCOMES-BASED ASSESSMENT PROGRAM REVIEW

Many faculty and administrators encounter points of resistance when they implement outcomes-based assessment program review. This resistance is normal; however, how you address the points of resistance or barriers may affect the genuineness and productivity of your outcomes-based assessment program review process positively or negatively. The following barriers to assessment are most typical. At some point all of the good practice program review institutions had to address these barriers; and some are still addressing them as new faculty and administrators cycle into leadership positions around their institutions, or as trustees, legislators, coordinating board members, alumni, parents, and students raise new policies and challenges.

The four most typical barriers to assessment (Bresciani, Frye, & Remlinger, in press) include

- limited time to conduct assessment;
- limited resources to put toward assessment;
- limited understanding of or expertise in assessment;
- perceived benefits of assessment are not substantial enough to engage in assessment; and
- not wanting to bother the students with completing several surveys.

While these may be the reasons that faculty and administrators report, further conversations reveal that the barriers can be summarized into two primary categories:

- Lack of understanding of the value and importance of outcomes-based assessment among those implementing it as well as among those top-level leadership who are being asked to support it
- Lack of resources to engage in meaningful and manageable assessment, which includes time to learn about and to engage in assessment, as well as having the institutional infrastructure to support it

The barriers that make up these two categories are many, and I discuss them in detail shortly.

As institutions instill outcomes-based assessment program review practices, these barriers and others must be addressed. Regardless of how many times you have heard excuses for why outcomes-based assessment program review is not being done, each barrier that a faculty member or administrator communicates to you is real, even though the institution may have already identified a strategy to address it. If your institution has not already identified a strategy to address the barrier, then your institution must do so. Or if your institution has already identified a strategy to address the barrier, and you feel that strategy has been communicated, then you may have to repackage the strategy to reveal the solution, or you may need more individualized strategies to assist the faculty or administrator. So, as a reminder, treat every barrier as if you never heard it before. There are solutions; you may just need to be very flexible and refine the solutions for the individual or program raising the concerns.

As we mentioned earlier, learning to engage in meaningful outcomes-based assessment program review is an educational process for the individual faculty and administrative members as well as for the institution as a whole. Paying attention to what and how faculty are learning how to improve their programs can formulate and refine your institutional expectations. This is an organic process. While expectations and structure need to be provided, it must be done in a manner that balances structure and flexibility. The harmony such a balance creates is intended to diminish faculty and staff anxiety surrounding institutional expectations while allowing faculty and staff the creativity and ingenuity to engage in learning more about what they do well and what they need to improve.

Flexibility in resolving barriers is not the only important criterion for moving faculty and staff forward; the ability to really understand the particular culture and listen to faculty and administrators is extremely important. A solution for one department may simply not work for another. So while sometimes it may be about repackaging a strategy, other times it means recommending a completely different solution to the program. For example, at Texas A&M University, faculty and researchers did not want to hear about outcomes-based assessment, so faculty and administrators charged with moving outcomes-based assessment program review forward repackaged it and called it evidence-based decision making. However, even with the repackaging, one group of prestigious researchers was still very resistant to the idea. For them, a different solution was needed.

An example of how to resolve this type of resistance was described in the keynote address given by a well-known member of the National Science Foundation (NSF) at the institution's annual assessment conference. The address focused on the integration of research and teaching. The NSF member drew from examples in funded grant research to illustrate the impact that new knowledge had in the classroom. Furthermore, the presentation illustrated how undergraduates could be engaged by discovering new knowledge in the classroom and through structured undergraduate research initiatives. Helping faculty see the connection between outcomes-based assessment in the classroom and research did not happen overnight, but this strategy, designed by one of the research faculty members, opened a new door.

The primary point here is that as you read through these barriers and the proposed solutions to them, keep in mind the principle we have espoused throughout this book" "No one size fits all"; each barrier experienced is unique, as is each strategy to address the barrier. This chapter seeks to generate ideas and to show you that barriers are normal and not to be feared. Further, if you purposefully implement strategies to answer the questions posed in chapter 5, and do so in a way that leverages your unique institutional culture, then many of the solutions will be readily available for addressing the barriers we pose in this chapter.

Lack of Understanding of Assessment

Addressing the lack of understanding of the value and importance of outcomes-based assessment often means to first address the "fear" that comes from a demand and knowing little or nothing about how to meet that demand. Often the solution to this fear is education and communication. Education about the unknown typically reduces one's fears. Even if new fears emerge as a result of the education, you are better informed and can address these new fears through conversations.

Keep in mind that you are working with professionals who are experts in their respective areas. Asking them to learn something very new and apply it to their area of expertise may be very intimidating to them. Their professional ego may feel at risk, and they may appear resistant simply because they fear failing to "get it."

As we mentioned earlier, there is a delicate balance between leaders' expectation that outcomes-based assessment will be completed and faculty and staff's belief that program review should be organic, genuine, meaningful, and manageable. Achieving this balance means that everyone has to know upfront what "outcomes-based assessment program review" means. Thus, generating a shared conceptual framework and common language may be an important first step in reducing fear of the process (see chapter 3).

If you have missed this first step and are off and running, you may have already articulated what "outcomes-based assessment," means, and all you need to do is communicate this meaning to the university community. Consider the collaborative approach that the Student Affairs Division at Oregon State University took once the division leadership committed to engaging in outcomes-based assessment:

Oregon State University: Student Affairs

At first many people in the division felt hesitant about and threatened by assessment. It conjured up visions of poor evaluation, dire consequences, and, ultimately, job loss. Thus, it was imperative from the beginning that people understand that the primary purpose of assessment and the subsequent evaluation of results would be used for program/service improvement. This message has continued to be delivered in a variety of ways as staffing has changed and this initiative has continued to evolve.

The cross-departmental makeup of the early assessment council was critical in developing credibility throughout the division, and the open invitation to join made it accessible to all levels within the division. In essence, anyone who had interest, energy, and a willingness to learn and lead was welcomed to the council. This practice of open membership and invitation, which has continued, has also allowed individuals to come and go with the understanding that the work would continue.

That early council set the tone and initial standards for assessment and how the structures would evolve and progress. Early in their work, the council members proposed a structure to support assessment in the division and to formalize the role of assessment in departmental reviews. While their recommendation was not acted on at the time, it did portend future developments. They also set the standard for sharing work and creating learning opportunities for anyone in the division. Hosting two campus-wide workshops where experts and novices alike shared their work with others served to continually increase organizational knowledge and commitment. (Submitted by Rebecca Sanderson and Larry Roper, Oregon State University)

Sometimes, faculty and staff need to understand how the results are going to be used even before they understand what assessment is all about. However, before answering the question, "how will the results be used?" in public, it may be wise to ensure that the person who can answer that question is well informed. Furthermore, there may be a logical progression within the answer to this question. For example, if faculty and staff are newly engaged in outcomes-based assessment program review, it may be wise to recommend initially that the results from outcomes-based assessment program review will inform decisions about improving the program. Later, it may be appropriate to feed those results to external reviewers (selected by the program's faculty) as Indiana University–Purdue University Indianapolis (IUPUI) does. Even later, depending on how programs are funded, it may be wise to use the results of program review to reallocate institutional funds. And, somewhere in between, it may be prudent to use the results to inform professional development needs.

Again, the emphasis here is that the institution must decide how the results are used. It may not be possible to determine how results will be used from the inception of the program, but most likely it will be decided as the process develops. Regardless, it is important to communicate to the university community how the results will be used and to be very consistent in implementing that decision. A program whose results are used for different purposes from what was communicated to the university community will cause the process to lose momentum.

One of the most effective ways to overcome fear is by building trust. If you are pretending to build a process that is organic and genuine, yet plan to use the information for purposes for which it was not intended, you will lose the trust of the very people from whom you are trying to gain it. As in the earlier analogy, it takes two people to climb, and it takes two people to dive. In both situations, you depend on your buddy to be there so you can climb on the mountain or go into the water. If your buddy does not do what he said he would do, you could risk serious injury or death. If you live to tell about how your buddy broke your trust, you certainly won't go climbing or diving with him again, and no doubt others will decide not to trust him, too. Worse, you may never even be able to enjoy the sport again. While this analogy may seem a bit melodramatic, consider the following. When you ask faculty and staff to engage in comprehensive outcomes-based assessment program review, you are asking them to become transparent in their day-to-day work. This transparency leaves them very vulnerable. If they can trust the decision makers to use the faculty and staff's articulated outcomes, evaluation methods, criteria, results, and recommendations with deliberate care, then they will continue to engage in outcomes-based assessment program review. Further, they will testify to their colleagues' trustworthiness, thus helping to expand the core of risk takers.

By now, you have recognized that the day-to-day "doers" of outcomes-based assessment are not the only ones who need to understand the purpose; top-level leaders expecting outcomes-based assessment program review also need to understand it and know how to use the results to inform their top-level decision making. Thus, top-level leaders create the need for another process for education and communication.

Indiana University–Purdue University Indianapolis: Top-Level Decision Makers

At Indiana University–Purdue University Indianapolis, we educate top-level leadership through involvement in the outcomes-based assessment program review process. When we invite reviewers to serve, we tell them that every member of the review team is expected to contribute at least one section to the final written report due within a month of the conclusion of the campus visit. Once the report is received in the office of the vice chancellor for planning and institutional improvement (PAII), it is disseminated to the campus chancellor, vice chancellors, dean or director of the unit reviewed, and department chair. We ask the chair or service unit head to work with colleagues to draft a considered response to each recommendation in the report and to send that to the vice chancellor for PAII within six months. A few conclusions and/or recommendations may be deemed inappropriate or impossible to implement, but each one should be addressed in the written response to the review compiled by the unit.

As soon as possible following receipt of the unit response, we ask the responsible dean or vice chancellor to schedule a discussion session that involves the dean of the faculties, if appropriate; the vice chancellor for PAII; the vice chancellor for graduate studies and research (if appropriate); the unit head; and faculty representatives, if desired. During this meeting, everyone concerned endeavors to find ways to support the unit in making warranted improvements.

During the third or fourth year following the unit review—approximately halfway between scheduled reviews—the unit head is invited to address the Program Review and Assessment Committee to report on progress in the unit since the review and on the quality of the review process itself. (Submitted by Trudy Banta and Karen Black, IUPUI)

Finally, it is also important to educate those providing infrastructure support to the process. If the infrastructure is not available to educate and support those involved in outcomes-based assessment program review—providing faculty workshops, individual consultations with departments, survey assistance, and so on—those involved in the process may receive insufficient or conflicting advice, or they may be unsure how to best provide for the process if they simply do not understand the purpose of the process. The majority of good practice institutions have committees that provide educational support to faculty and staff engaged in outcomes-based assessment program review. New Jersey City University is progressively engaged in the professional development provided to the key faculty and staff involved in directing and supporting this process. This support allows the team to incorporate new ideas as its members move the institution to improve the self-reflection process. (For more information on New Jersey City University's process see http://styluspub.com/resources/outcomes-basedprogramreview .aspx.)

Another strategy to help faculty and staff understand what the process is really about is to engage in a faculty- or staff-dependent model. This model is referred to as a faculty-dependent model because the entire outcomes-based assessment process depends on faculty leadership to take the researched theories and adapt them to the unique institutional or program culture. Rather than having a process driven without research from the assessment field, the faculty-dependent model implies that the professionals hired to coordinate the outcomes-based assessment program review are the ones who conduct the research on what is working well at the institution and who pay attention to what is working well elsewhere.

This strategy addresses two primary barriers. First, for faculty who do not understand outcomes-based assessment, it provides a professional who can share good practices that save them time and frustration. Second, since faculty have saved some time by not having to do the research, the faculty committee can consider options, select one or several, and apply them to its own institutional culture. Without this last step, assessment quickly becomes an administratively driven process and loses effectiveness. The beauty of this model is that it offers the opportunity for faculty to educate all and be educated.

Comprehensive faculty and staff development initiatives are important in educating faculty about the assessment process and in supporting them throughout the process. Hampden-Sydney organized extensive professional development programs when it prepared its faculty to deliver and evaluate writing proficiency. Keystone College's faculty development initiatives emerged as the college learned how to refine majors while engaged in outcomes-based assessment program review.

In attempting to overcome assessment barriers, you may often hear that faculty and staff need to become more involved. Often they are not involved because they do not understand the value of being involved. Answering the questions posed in chapter 5 and using the strategies in this chapter may help build faculty understanding of assessment and, therefore, may increase faculty and staff involvement in assessment. To illustrate the application of several strategies mentioned earlier, consider the following good practice institution example:

New Jersey City University

New Jersey City University is a diverse urban institution classified as Hispanic Serving and as a Minority Institution. In addition, a significant portion of enrolled students identify themselves as immigrants. The College of Professional Studies is one of three colleges within the university, and approximately 80 percent of its faculty are tenured. The university also has a strong union. Supporting nontenured faculty, innovation, and change requires innovative approaches.

During a four-year period, faculty development opportunities in the College of Professional Studies were identified that would introduce a broad spectrum of teaching and learning concepts, applications, and strategies. One of the goals of these activities was to build a pedagogical body of knowledge that would help transform a "faculty-centered" learning enterprise into one that was more "student-centered." In addressing faculty philosophy and practice, the intent was to create an environment in which student and program assessment become hallmarks of excellence. Student assessment gained momentum, particularly with the development of university-wide competencies (i.e., oral and written communication, quantitative reasoning, technology, critical thinking, and information literacy). However, program assessment met with resistance, because faculty did not understand what "assessment" meant. There was no university-wide policy or procedures outlining requirements for program review, and there was a daunting need for many faculty within a department to coordinate and plan.

Because modeling behavior is an effective means of promoting behavior change, it was determined that working with a few small programs and with faculty who were particularly open to program assessment would be a better way to achieve our goal. Consequently, we invited all faculty to participate in an initiative, called the "Centers of Excellence." Seven individuals responsible for coordinating small (vis à vis student enrollment and faculty) or emerging programs responded (B.S., Fire Science; B.S., Security; M.S., Accounting; M.S., Finance; M.S., Health Sciences/School Nursing; B.S., Travel and Tourism). The B.S. Travel and Tourism faculty later withdrew from the project.

Their first task was to establish (and prioritize) criteria characteristic of program excellence. Using Middle States guidelines, participants identified *standards* of excellence and *elements* of those standards. The following is the result of their work:

Center of Excellence:
Standards and Elements

A Center of Excellence

Standard 1:

Espouses a vision that incorporates research, creativity, and shared values.

Elements:
    a. Mission
    b. Vision

    c. Goals

    d. Values

    e. Strategic plan

Standard 2:

Challenges students to meet or exceed *rigorous professional standards.*

  Elements:

    a. Intellectually stimulating

    b. Ongoing assessment (student, program, and five-year review)

    c. Challenging curriculum

    d. High expectations

    e. Performance-based

    f. Accreditation, if appropriate

Standard 3:

Establishes a learner-centered environment *in which students have input about what and how they learn and where they develop and realize their own potential in a collegial and flexibly structured environment. Academic, personal, and professional growth focuses on the opportunity to gain experience based on what is relevant to learners as practitioners.*

  Elements:

    a. Student ownership and responsibility

    b. Focus on students

    c. Student engagement

    d. Active learners/participants

Standard 4:

Embraces diversity in an environment of equality and opportunity, where differences in cultures, backgrounds, and ideas are valued and integrated.

  Elements:

    a. Cultural "competence"

    b. Diversity as a valuable resource

Standard 5:

Expects faculty to incorporate *high standards and demonstrate excellence* in the areas of teaching, lifelong learning, service, and research.

Elements:

    a. Scholar practitioners
    b. Responsive to stakeholder needs
    c. Accomplished in professional field
    d. Committed to excellence in teaching and learning
    e. Committed to service

[Several standards have been removed for this publication due to space constraints, but they may be found on the NJCU website.]

The second task required establishing mission and vision statements and goals for each program consistent with those of the university. Each individual representing a program (and working in conjunction with colleagues outside the group) provided statements to the Centers of Excellence faculty. This work was critically reviewed and modified.

The third task involved determining ways in which each of the elements (objectives) could be measured and assessed. The first phase of this task involved inventorying assessment measures and activities currently in place. This phase has been completed, and the next phase, identifying means of measurement for all objectives, has been completed as well.

Program coordinators are not responsible for reporting on all elements (objectives) the initial semester, but they will work instead with objectives that are most meaningfully related to the goals of their respective programs. Feedback (data and information) from each measure is analyzed to determine what modifications may be required, and how the change will be implemented is explained. At the conclusion of each semester, an outcomes report is completed.

Finally, after an assessment of the "Centers of Excellence" assessment plan in its entirety, changes will be recommended and acted upon. (Submitted by S. Bloomberg, C. Chew, L. Chewey, M. Ettinger, K. Malley, M. McDonald, R. Overton, J. Riotto, B. Soo Hoo, New Jersey City University)

In structuring an approach to program assessment in this manner, faculty receive support from their fellow program coordinators (constituting, in essence, a learning community within a learning community) and are encouraged to select from various elements (objectives) that are particularly relevant to their respective programs. The process also calls for "phasing in" of a program assessment plan over a period that is determined by the particular faculty coordinator and his or her colleagues. Following an assessment of the work of the first cohort, a second cohort of faculty (and programs) will be invited to participate for the 2005–06 academic year.

Faculty and staff need additional support to encourage them to become more involved in assessment, that is, day-to-day reporting and consultation services. At Oregon State University, the Director of Assessment for Student Affairs, along with the entire "trained" Assessment Council is available to provide feedback on assessment plans and reports.

At North Carolina State and at Truman State universities, a central office provides faculty and staff with an easy-to-access portal to query institutional and survey data. This allows faculty and staff to get quick reads on program progress so that they can delve further into more meaningful and specific outcomes-based assessment.

At IUPUI Planning and Institutional Improvement (PAII), institutional staff are the principal providers of support for program review. First, each unit is on a seven-year review schedule. Then they convene a meeting of the responsible vice chancellor(s), dean, and unit head to discuss the issues to be addressed in the unit self-study, during the campus visit by the reviewers, and in the reviewers' written report.

A decade ago, PAII staff created a step-by-step *Program Review Timeline* that begins twelve to eighteen months before the reviewers' visit and extends two months beyond the date of the visit. The timeline includes forty-four steps, along with how much time before or after the reviewers' visit each step should take place and the person(s) responsible. Each responsible party receives a copy of this document to see what needs to be done and when. More recently, one-page summaries of responsibilities for deans/vice chancellors and unit heads have been developed to go along with the more detailed timeline, which combines everyone's responsibilities in a single listing.

Following soon after the planning session, PAII staff visit the unit to be reviewed to discuss the types of information to be provided from central sources to augment the unit's self-study. For over a decade, IUPUI Office of Information Management and Institutional Research staff have administered surveys to enrolled students and alumni. Unit data can be compared with schoolwide and campus averages. Since 2000, the National Survey of Student Engagement (NSSE) has been given to IUPUI students every other year, and now students' responses are available for selected units. Numerous campus performance indicators, such as persistence rates and numbers of graduates in various racial and ethnic groups over time, are available. Since IUPUI requires that each responsibility center balance its own income and expenditures each year, activity-based costing data showing the differential costs of various initiatives have become an increasingly valued resource.

PAII staff work with each unit to the extent requested—providing unique data sets, furnishing examples of data displays and self-studies created by other IUPUI units, and commenting on early drafts of the self-study. Staff also arrange for reviewers' travel and accommodations. Up to two months before the review team visits, PAII staff work with all concerned to create and disseminate a schedule that will bring the reviewers in contact with virtually every office on campus that can provide an informed perspective on the unit under review. PAII staff furnish and/or monitor all logistics during the campus visit to ensure that the schedule proceeds smoothly.

Following the reviewers' visit, PAII staff follow up to ensure that the reviewers' report comes in on time. They disseminate the report to all who need to see it, monitor the unit's response to the review, and arrange the follow-up meeting with all who are responsible for the review to give everyone an opportunity to support the unit in taking appropriate responsive action. After three years, PAII staff schedule a presentation by the unit head to PRAC members concerning the long-term impact of the review and suggestions for improving the review process. (Submitted by Trudy Banta and Karen Black, IUPUI)

At Texas A&M University, the Center for Teaching Excellence leads faculty development initiatives, while the Student Life Studies office leads professional development for the Student Affairs Division, and the Office of Institutional Assessment leads assessment professional development efforts for the other administrative units. To make sure that all of the offices are teaching similar concepts, they collaborate on workshop designs and simultaneously host integrated workshops. New Jersey City University and Alverno College provide the majority of their faculty and staff development through their faculty and staff leadership committees.

In the examples above, you saw the intermingling of educational initiatives with educational support. There are built-in feedback loops or intentionally designed meta-assessment processes to ensure that the experiences and perspectives of faculty and staff are intermingled with improvements made to the program review process. Implementation of outcomes-based assessment program review is iterative and cyclical. To maintain meaning to faculty and staff and to increase their involvement, the program review process must be refined as often as the faculty and staff need for it to be. No good practice institution has the program review process that it began with. In all cases, each institution has refined its process, and no institution will tell you that it has already "arrived." Each expects and aspires to refine the process further.

If you want to determine where your institution is in regard to faculty and staff involvement in assessing student learning, it may be valuable to pose the following questions, taken from *Improving Institutional Practice*, published in 2004 by the Council of Regional Accrediting Commissions.

1. How much emphasis is given to commitment to student learning as part of faculty hiring?
2. In the evaluation of faculty, how much importance is given to their effectiveness in producing learning outcomes?
3. Where is a focus on learning evident in key institutional documents, such as the college catalog, program descriptions, and personnel policies?
4. In what ways does the institution encourage and disseminate innovations in teaching and learning, and discuss their implications for curriculum and pedagogy?
5. How congruent are instructional techniques and delivery systems with students' capabilities and learning needs?
6. In what ways are faculty members incorporating research on student learning in their teaching?
7. To what extent do educational offerings provide an opportunity for students to engage each other and their teachers in a free exchange of ideas and attitudes? [In] active student engagement in learning? [In] an opportunity for collaborative learning?
8. What is the congruence between learning goals and assessment practices? To what degree does the institution engage in "assessment of learning," that is, ongoing assessment with feedback to help students improve?
9. To what degree is the institution's assessment program marked by faculty ownership, and used in ways that lead to educational improvements? [By] feedback to faculty on a regular basis useful for

the improvement of instruction and learning? [By] incentives, rec-
ognitions, and rewards for faculty efforts in assessment?

10. Does the institution award degrees and certificates based on student
achievement of a program's stated learning outcomes? (pp. 24–27)

You may continue to hear from certain faculty and staff that they are
"confused" by what you are asking them to do. Even after attending workshops and hearing explanations of what outcomes-based assessment program
review is and why it is important, they may claim they still "don't get it."
While their confusion may be real, investigate further to see if their confusion is a strategy. Some faculty and administrators have been known to claim
they are confused simply to keep you finding varying ways to teach them
how to do it, while they passively resist engaging in the self-reflection
process.

Another reason that faculty use to avoid engaging in outcomes-based
assessment is that they fear it violates academic freedom. Academic freedom
has never implied a lack of quality assurance; therefore, those who claim that
outcomes-based assessment program review is in conflict with academic freedom do not understand that their colleagues have every right to demand a
certain level of excellence in their students' learning. Excellence in student
learning can be demanded without telling a faculty member how to achieve
or evaluate it. Such a demand is not a violation of academic freedom (AAUP,
1970).

Lack of Resources to Engage in Meaningful and Manageable Assessment

Some institutions believe they cannot engage in outcomes-based assessment
program review because they do not have enough resources. To believe that
engagement in meaningful outcomes-based assessment program review does
not require resources would be a farce. It does; and the first, most precious
resource required is time.

Time: To say that implementation and refinement of outcomes-based
assessment program review processes does not require time and energy from
faculty and staff is simply inaccurate. It does require time—time to educate
faculty and staff about the process and how to engage in it meaningfully;
time to reflect purposefully on the results of it; and time to document the

findings, decisions made, plans for improvement in the program, for the review process, and for follow-up after the evaluation on the newly made decisions and practices.

As we all know, additional time cannot be created; it can only be reallocated. Time to engage in outcomes-based assessment program review must be reallocated from doing something else (Bresciani et al., 2004). Many good practice institutions have made this reallocation. In some cases, it was simply a matter of calling what faculty and staff were already doing "assessment." In many cases, faculty and staff were already engaged in outcomes-based assessment; they just did not know they were. Thus, the process just needed to be named, and the resulting decisions and planning documented.

In other cases, faculty and staff had to be asked to reallocate time from their current work to reflection and planning for their work (Bresciani et al., 2004). In other words, some staff did not need to plan twenty-five programs, but could plan ten and use the time that had been allocated to planning the additional fifteen to evaluating the ten. For some faculty, it meant not trying to cover so much content in their courses or finding more efficient ways of doing so (Suskie, 2004), and building means of assessing whether students could apply the content that was learned (Maki, 2004). For still others, it meant documenting the inherent graduate review process and articulating the learning and research outcomes.

For others who could not reduce programming or services, it meant starting small by planning to evaluate one service component every year and using that time to build evaluation of the service component into day-to-day administration. Thus, the evaluation process becomes a "habit" (Bresciani et al., 2004), and the administrative unit can move on to the next year and the next service to evaluate, having already established some reflection and assessment habits.

In many good practice institutions, the expectation was made clear that assessment is not an "add-on"—that program review is not a process that is set aside, to be thought of only once every five, seven, or ten years. It should be a process of reflection that is built into day-to-day work. In this model, time is not taken away from teaching, it is invested in improving teaching. Time is not taken away from providing services, it is invested in improving services. Time is not taken away from discipline research, the research informs the design and assessment of student learning. And for some disciplines and administrative units, outcomes-based assessment is research; it is considered to be their discipline scholarship.

Given the necessity of reallocating time, the time needed to document outcomes-based assessment program review processes and results is indeed daunting. As we all know, it is one thing to take four hours to process what we are learning about our program with our colleagues and plan for the improvements; it is another to then produce a written summary of that discussion. Such documentation is new to many, so it is often difficult to "find" the time to document. However, without documentation of outcomes-based assessment program review, no one would know that your institution is engaged in it. There would be no way of knowing how the process has helped you improve student learning, teaching, services, and research. Without documentation, these good practice institutions would not have been able to share their lessons learned and examples of excellence.

Documentation: Documentation of this process is necessary, so time must be allocated for it. If it does not occur, the memory of how an improvement was made may be lost. To illustrate, consider that if researchers did not write summaries of their findings, we would have nothing to pass on to the next generation to inform additional research and to build on past findings. The same is true for program delivery and teaching curriculum. If an institution does not document its program review, it cannot share this information to improve services. Furthermore, cross-discipline and cross-division conversations are hindered, as there is no report to read to prepare for the conversations and no summary of findings to debate in regard to the next course of action. The institutional memory of excellence becomes lost with the passing of an administration if program review findings are not documented and used.

Documentation takes time, so it can be a significant barrier to engaging in systematic outcomes-based assessment. The extent to which institutions can provide assistance in this area is important. Some institutions provide online documentation tools; others provide administrative support staff to assist with writing up findings and decisions. Again, these resources may be valuable; however, use them with caution, as many faculty and administrators can quickly turn providing aid for documentation into a one-size-fits-all solution, rather than demonstrating purposeful reflection in their documentation practices.

Faculty and Staff Development: In addition to time, another valuable resource required for outcomes-based assessment is investment in faculty and staff to enable them to learn about how to meaningfully engage in this process, given all the demands of their work. We have spent a great deal of time discussing this necessary resource, and we have used the analogy that you wouldn't expect your students to be able to conduct a lab experiment effectively without first teaching them how; thus, you cannot expect faculty and administrators to engage in this inquiry process without first teaching them how.

To illustrate the value of providing faculty and staff development, we have shared examples from good practice institutions, along with questions to pose to your own institution about how well faculty and staff are prepared to embrace and implement outcomes-based assessment program review. All that said, without institutionalized efforts to embed outcomes-based assessment education into faculty and staff development programs, an institution should not expect faculty and staff to understand what outcomes-based assessment program review is, let alone know how to engage in it in practical and meaningful ways. Implementation of a systematic, institution-wide faculty and staff development program will empower you to address many barriers that arise when delivering this type of program review. Providing incentives for faculty to take the time to engage in these faculty development opportunities is also important.

Other Resources: In previous chapters, we have mentioned other resources of good practice institutions for engaging in outcomes-based assessment program review. To reiterate, faculty and staff need access to readily available

- Institutional research data. In many instances where faculty and staff have to run their own analysis just to determine enrollment trends, first-year academic preparedness data, or simple biodemographic makeup of their cohorts, faculty and staff are taking valuable time away from reflecting on what the data mean to their program outcomes. Thus, if faculty and staff can have data query analysis tools to apply to the already organized extracts of data from the institutional transactional systems (i.e., non-privacy-protected fields from the student information system, human resource system, and financial systems), they can quickly access the information they need to inform their program planning and evaluation needs.
- Institutional survey data. Similar to research data, providing faculty and staff with institutionally designed, administered, and analyzed surveys will give them with much needed information for program

review that will allow them to focus on the meaning of the results and their application to program improvement. Furthermore, the ability of the programs to use the results of the surveys, as well as the institutional empirical data, will enable faculty and staff to improve the institutional data collection processes.

- Web resources and templates. With increasing access to websites, programs can place many of the documents they used to compile in their program review three-ring paper binder on the Web instead. Doing so means spending less time finding out who has the last version of the mission statement and spending more time on determining whether the departmental mission statement is still representative of the program. Other documents historically collected in the binder—such as faculty curriculum vitas and staff resumes, course syllabi and program agendas, utilization statistics, service and customer satisfaction policies, and rules and regulations—can be placed on the Web and updated easily. Placing these documents on the Web means more people can access and discuss them in relation to program review findings. Departmental websites provide living documentation for the outcomes-based assessment process; they allow for items to be updated easily and used for inclusive discussions.

- Online resources. Ephraim Schechter, formerly of North Carolina State University and University of Colorado-Boulder, has pulled together a comprehensive online assessment resource library for administrators and faculty engaged in all aspects of outcomes-based assessment program review—see http://www2.acs.ncsu.edu/UPA/assmt/resource.htm. Simply linking to this site or the portions of it that your institution would find most helpful to your conceptual framework for outcomes-based assessment program review will provide free, easy-to-access, helpful resources for faculty and staff development.

- Survey development tools. Many technological tools aid in the design, administration, and analysis of surveys. While survey methodology is only one of the many methodologies available to outcomes-based assessment program review, providing faculty and staff with tools to help them quickly and easily design means to gather information about their program's effectiveness allows them to reallocate time to reflecting on what they are finding, rather than to gathering much-needed information.

- Assessment plan and report consultation, including all aspects of the outcomes-based assessment process. In addition to faculty and staff development programs providing one-on-one consultation on all aspects of outcomes-based assessment—including writing outcomes, selecting research methodologies and assessment tools, interpreting results, and writing reports—they will ease faculty and staff anxieties about program review and allow them to focus their energies on discerning what the process means for their program improvement. The same is true for the following one-on-one consultation services:
  - course development
  - project/activity development
  - program development
  - course or project mapping
  - evaluation method selection
  - tips on writing outcomes
  - tips on analyzing and interpreting data
  - tips on presenting results

- Professional development. In addition to internal institutional faculty and staff development programs, faculty and staff must engage in their own discipline's professional development opportunities. Doing so allows them to influence and be influenced by standards in their discipline. They can bring these new understandings back to their own campus, apply them to their program review processes, and excel further in their discipline and professional areas.

- Opportunities to present outcomes-based assessment program review findings. Similar to provision of professional development opportunities with the faculty or staff discipline mentioned above, providing the opportunity to present outcomes-based assessment program review findings at conferences helps teach others about the value of engaging in such review. Further, such presentations encourage feedback from conference participants about how they can improve their review process. Publicly sharing findings and methodology can be mutually beneficial to everyone involved.

- Opportunities to publish outcomes-based assessment program review findings.

- Opportunities to engage in conversations about program review discoveries within the institution. Establishing a regular forum for information exchange or poster sessions can set the stage for such conversations.
- Documentation tools. As we mentioned earlier, documentation is time-consuming. Providing electronic tools that aid in the documentation process saves faculty and staff time, while reinforcing that they can use purposeful and meaningful documentation of outcomes-based assessment for professional accreditation purposes, grant writing, institutional accreditation, and legislative and trustee reports as well as for program and institutional marketing and recruitment of students, faculty, and staff.
- Grants. Good practice institutions have found providing institutional grants to aid programs in starting up their outcomes-based assessment program review processes to be very valuable. However, the point at which programs are expected to become less reliant on institutional grants and embed the costs of the review process into their own departmental budgets is often a touchy transition that requires time and patience to negotiate.
- Release time. Similar to providing institutional grants, providing release time to faculty and staff to begin planning for outcomes-based assessment program review may be extremely valuable, if not essential. The transition process from release time to no release time may be as challenging as the movement away from providing institutional grants.
- Faculty and administrative fellows. Similar to providing release time or institutional grants, using faculty and administrative fellows is becoming more common. The intent is to hire or buy out a certain percentage of time for one faculty member per college or for a division administrator to provide the faculty and staff support for educating everyone within that division or college about assessment. This practice is often a train-the-trainer model and can be adopted by an organization as finances permit. For example, you might consider funding a faculty fellow for one college who is preparing to meet professional accreditation standards through outcomes-based assessment program review. Then, as the other colleges institute programs preparing for accreditation, you can phase in the financing of their fellows as well.

These resources do require investment of institutional or college and division funds. How your institution chooses to approach the investment planning is for your institutional and program review leadership to determine, with your guidance and recommendations. Not to acknowledge that resources are required, whether it be reallocation of centralized institutional resources or decentralized provision of the resources, is unwise and may hinder advancement of your own institution's excellence.

Whether your institution is just beginning to implement outcomes-based assessment program review or is in the process of refining a long-standing process, reviewing the resources committed to outcomes-based assessment program review is a good idea. A sample plan for resources and inclusion of appropriate faculty and staff development for the outcomes-based assessment review process can be found at http://assessment.tamu.edu/StrategicPlanningforEBDM.html. Each institution should have its own plan for developing its internal resources to support outcomes-based assessment program review, and each one should proceed within its own means and capabilities.

Again, there is no one right way to approach this conversation. There is no one right way to provide the institutional resources that are recommended or that your institution recognizes as required to engage in meaningful and manageable outcomes-based assessment program review. However, it is important that your institution engage in purposeful planning of what is needed to model a learning organization (Senge, 1990).

7

RECOMMENDATIONS FOR FUTURE CONSIDERATIONS FOR IMPLEMENTING OUTCOMES-BASED ASSESSMENT PROGRAM REVIEW COMPONENTS AND EVALUATING THEIR EFFECTIVENESS

This book has focused on good practices for implementing outcomes-based assessment program review. While I have posed many barriers and proposed strategies to overcome those barriers, several key concerns remain. While I struggle with the question of what the future of higher education will look like and how we will know that quality is evident, it is my hope that outcomes-based assessment, if put into systematic and meaningful practice, will continue to aid in transforming higher education and improving the quality of student learning and development, research, and service. Questions such as the ones that follow should be researched further: Are institutions truly centered on student learning? Are they funded in a manner that allows them to be learning-centered? Do their organizational structures and rewards systems promote student learning? How will we know excellence has been achieved in all aspects? What will it look like? Will institutions of higher education truly be transformed into learner-centered institutions as a result of outcomes-based assessment program review?

From the outset I have felt a responsibility to share with others what we have learned from many wonderful scholars and practitioners; some are named in this book, and many other are emerging. My hope is that readers will come away with the understanding that outcomes-based assessment program review should avoid focusing on process for process's sake but, rather, should focus on implementing new habits of self-reflection and informed decision making—all in an effort to transform how we talk about quality of higher education and definitely to transform how we identify it.

Many higher education scholars worry that our time is running out to demonstrate through organized and systematic outcomes-based assessment program review that what we do in institutions of higher education is improving, that we are student-learning centered, and that what we do day to day is of quality (personal communication at the National Meeting on the Future of Assessment in Costa Rica, 2005). We understand what these scholars are saying. However, we are concerned that it may remain difficult to find means to appease external constituency demands for accountability when the very nature of what is required to be reported could be disrupting institutions' ability to report what does have value in conversations about quality of higher education.

For example, IPEDS (Integrated Postsecondary Education Data System) requires several specific measurements from institutions of higher education, none of which focuses on indicators of quality of education—at least not in a manner that identifies where improvements can be made to enhance learning in academic programs or to enhance discipline-specific research, for example. How does number of credit hours equate to improved learning? Credit hours, among other traditional modes of delivering and managing higher education, are truly outdated (Wellman, 2005). We still have no evidence that the number of credit hours offered in a particular subject area contributes to quality of learning in that area. Rather, learning is identified by course flow, curriculum design, pedagogical delivery, and attention to how students are learning. Can the same amount of learning occur in a three-credit-hour course as in a six-credit-hour course if the learning is carefully constructed and designed with the diversity of learners in mind?

Moving further along these lines, why are empirical measures called for? Is it too much to ask higher-level decision makers to actually read a summary report of qualitative indicators of excellence in higher education? Why does evidence of effectiveness always have to be presented in easy-to-digest pictures, graphs, and bullet points? How can we possibly create meaningful conversations around that kind of summative, descriptive, empirical data? How can institutional excellence and access to higher education be preserved if all institutions are required only to have comparable data?

We recognize that there is value in being able to "benchmark" indicators of quality. Yet, in our efforts to benchmark and compare, have we diminished the meaning of the very nature of understanding how students learn and develop? Why do we not compare grade reports of Introduction to Micro-Economics courses across the hundreds of higher education institutions to identify quality learning? Because we know that many of the factors that contribute to these grades are not the same. For example,

1. student learning outcomes for each course may not be the same;
2. the framework for what is taught is not the same;
3. the preparation of the students for each class is not the same, nor is the expertise of each of the faculty members;
4. faculty's ability to apply their research to the classroom curriculum is not the same, and their research is not the same;
5. the pedagogy is different; and
6. the assignments, and the means to evaluate them, are different.

We know these grades are not comparable indicators, unless faculty members met and agreed on learning outcomes, delivery, means to evaluate, application of their research to the classroom, and so on, yet some states have set up articulation agreements espousing that learning will be the same in this three-credit-hour course at this institution as it is in courses similar to this at other institutions.

Would we rather hold each institution to a high level of scrutiny for the quality of self-review the institution is undertaking and hold it accountable for the transparency of such self-review? For example, if we as a nation are genuinely serious about the integrity of our self-review standards, why don't we improve our self-review process and be held accountable for it by our regional accreditors? Isn't this already happening? you ask. We think so, but how can regional accreditors be empowered to move forward and reinforce requirements for high-quality self-evaluation?

We recognize that making self-review processes too transparent too early in the game can undermine the institutional integrity of objective review practices; however, in time, shouldn't we be able to expect that every institution would include on its website each academic program's student learning outcomes as well as how students are performing collectively in each of those outcomes? Wouldn't we also want to be able to demonstrate what each program's administrators and faculty are doing to improve the performance for each outcome? And wouldn't it be interesting to know whether stakeholders are willing to finance such improvements?

> Think of it in this way, rather than understanding whether your son or daughter or niece or nephew will get a good quality education based on an institution's faculty to student ratio (e.g., easy to identify indicators), wouldn't it be great to actually know what your student would be expected to learn in any specific major and what the level of learning within that major was for students who came before? And if you are wondering why the level of student learning is what it is, you could look deeper to see what the plans for improving the learning are at each institution and how they will be financed. You may then realize a progressive institution striving to achieve more may be better suited to your student than one that had already established itself. This kind of data could transcend legacy reputations and allow institutions to compete for international and national students based on the facts and the end results of learning regardless of how well the student was prepared when she entered. (Bresciani, 2005, p. 1)

In addition, such transparency gives those who fund higher education reforms more information to inform their decisions and provides the public with accountability to inform donors' and other supporters' decisions. Think of how helpful it would be to have an informed discussion where proposed reductions in funding correlate with a decrease in student performance based on an understanding of student learning *and* development as *defined and identified by the faculty or administrators responsible for the program.*

Major transformations are needed for higher education to benefit fully from the purposeful reflection brought about by outcomes-based assessment program review. The following elements describe just a few of the potentially necessary transformations.

1. Key leadership of institutions of higher education must demonstrate that they genuinely care about student learning issues. This is not to say that they do not demonstrate this concern in isolation

from other concerns regarding research productivity, community engagement, and even athletics. It is possible to balance these concerns, but university leadership must be held to a level of serious accountability for balancing them. Governing boards of institutions must hold university leaders accountable for this kind of thinking. How do we educate university leaders about the importance of formative frameworks for improving all they do, and do so in a manner in which learning is central to the operation of the university?

2. A culture of trust and integrity must be created at institutions through consistent actions of university leaders who demonstrate a commitment to ethical and quality evidence-based decision making. For outcomes-based assessment program review to take hold and become systematic and pervasive, university leaders must use the evidence gathered from outcomes-based assessment program review in a manner that promotes organizational learning. Senge (1990) writes that an organization that links "adaptive learning" with "generative learning" increases its capacity to learn and, therefore, also increases its capacity to improve and reinvent itself. If universities demonstrate for themselves that they are the learning organizations that embody the qualities they desire to instill in their students, if the institution embodies Papert's (1991) constructionist learning epistemology, the institution will use objectively gathered information on how to improve itself and do so in a consistent manner that acknowledges human contributions and provides for professional development opportunities. In this manner, over time, the institution's culture can become one of trust and integrity for truth seeking, rather than one where staff are concerned about their lack of accomplishments in their unit, causing them to worry about job loss rather than trying to identify opportunities for professional development.

3. We must reconstruct our mental models for delivering higher education so that we can overcome our administrative delivery limitations. Why do the majority of our higher education institutions still deliver education in sixteen-week modules and design learning in terms of credit hours rather than competencies? Can we learn from the role model of Western Governors University (Johnstone, 2005) and apply that learning to reforming our institutional structures so

that learning is enhanced? Can we learn to focus more on identifying whether we have achieved the desired outcomes rather than
counting the number of credit hours offered or the number of
weeks in a term?

4. We have to connect formative assessment with summative assessment and link discussion of improvement with discussions on accountability. We have to connect the somewhat competing worlds
   of expectations for learning, or at least for the accountability of that
   student learning within federal and state governments, institutional
   boards of trustees, higher-level institutional administration, and faculty. Often, expectations for accountability of learning appear to
   compete with the ability of faculty to focus on improving student
   learning, because the requested indicators do not help to inform
   specific decisions for improving student learning and development.
   High-level decision makers appear to value easy-to-digest numbers,
   which may not provide faculty with the specific information they
   need for improving courses and curriculum.

5. We must emphasize the connection of curriculum design, pedagogical approaches, and faculty development to delivery and evaluation
   of student learning. Somewhere along the way, we came to value
   individual expertise and lost the connection of that expertise,
   whether it is embodied in research, teaching, or service, to the learning that was taking place in the classroom and outside the classroom. We must link individual experts and collections of experts
   to the overall plan for learning within programs, departments, and
   colleges. In addition, we must develop individual experts so they
   know how best to apply their expertise for the optimum learning
   experience for the student, regardless of whether it occurs in the
   classroom, the lab, outside the classroom, or in the internship or
   practicum.

6. We need to rethink our internal and external rewards system. With
   the understanding that rewards for research will never go away, nor
   should they, how do we better connect rewards for research and
   rewards for teaching? Do we set up a separate rewards system—one
   for research and one for teaching? Or do we strive to better connect
   research to both the classroom and the out-of-classroom learning
   experiences?

More difficult in this conversation is the challenge that institutions have historically celebrated and promoted faculty as individual commodities. We have historically promoted faculty for their individual contributions as researchers, for their individual service records, or for their individual teaching performances. There are very few avenues to reward the group work that it takes to team teach, to develop multidisciplinary approaches to learning, to integrate the curricular and the co-curricular, to redesign curriculum, or to embed inquiry practices or other effective pedagogies into day-to-day work. We do not have readily available avenues to celebrate such collaborative work, and the improvement of student learning is a collaborative process. Rather, we depend on the faculty's intrinsic concern with improving student learning. While many are concerned, they invest in this at risk to their own professional career.

7. We must consider how our models for delivering external accountability in the United States affect our ability to speak coherently and confidently about the quality of higher education in the United States. Since we have no Ministry of Higher Education per se, we count on the states to identify the quality of higher education in the country as a whole. Some states have organized themselves or are organizing themselves so they can address this question. However, others are not. While states may continue to gather institutional performance indicator data such as persistence and graduation rates, these types of data often are collected without regard to institutional type, mission, and focus. In addition, they say very little about the quality of learning at the institutions.

Our inability to collectively talk about the quality of higher education in the United States frustrates the public and their elected representatives. This frustration is heightened by other countries' ability to demonstrate genuine quality in student learning in great detail. For example, Australia's Quality Assurance Agency has a good practice database, which provides detailed illustrations of quality practice in the country's institutions of higher education. These good practices are identified by extensive peer reviews and posted on the agency's website to serve as illustrations for others (for more information, see http://www.auqa.edu.au/gp/index.php).

8. We must reframe our graduate programs that prepare our experts for the academy to prepare them to teach and evaluate the effectiveness of their teaching as well. If we could insert into each graduate program a few modules that taught graduate students how to teach effectively and evaluate the effectiveness of student learning, we would most likely be one step closer to embedding this practice into the culture of higher education. As it is now, we depend on elective teaching assistant training to cover this important aspect. Often, teacher assistant training is one to two hours and, possibly, one to two days. Furthermore, this training is often done with newly arrived graduate students, who have very little time and attention to commit to the training and no time to revise syllabi or pedagogy before they begin teaching the course themselves. In addition, teacher assistants typically are left on their own after the beginning of the semester to seek the additional feedback required to improve their teaching and, consequently, student learning. If we could instill pedagogical practice, curriculum design, and evaluation of student learning principles into graduate preparation programs as a requirement with intentional follow-up, we would most likely be ahead of our own learning curve.

9. We must consider how we finance higher education and how the allocation of the financing may hinder conversations that surround improvement of student learning. Often, when institutions, particularly public institutions, receive funding, they receive it based on head count, seat time, or credit-hour production. These models do not recognize quality of student learning, nor do they recognize the cost differentials for improving student learning or embedding faculty research expertise in the curriculum. Therefore, institutions can continue to receive funding regardless of how well or how much students are learning.

Even if the governing agencies continue to allocate resources based on numbers, institutions could distribute those monies to programs based on quality and desired means to influence quality paying particular attention to cost differentials for improved pedagogy. For example, if my institution has a thousand students and ten programs, and I get $100 per student, I have $100,000 to fund ten programs. One way to allocate the money to the programs is to divide it by students enrolled in each program. An alternative would be to ask each program to evaluate its quality of learning. I could then award the resources to programs that have (1) engaged in quality evaluation and (2) identified means for improvement. Additional criteria to help the allocation would be based on what we are trying to accomplish as an institution, and to award the funds to those units better prepared to move us forward with our institutional mission without sacrificing quality in a pertinent area such as general education or Americans with Disabilities Act (ADA) compliance.

This kind of funding formula may encourage faculty and staff to engage actively in evaluating and improving their programs as they see resources being tied to recommendations for improvement.

10. We need to consider a model that hires faculty and administrators with the explicit expectation that they will engage in genuine outcomes-based assessment. I have spoken to many faculty who believe they were not hired to teach, let alone evaluate the performance of their students in the classroom, lab, or co-curricular. Thus, when they find out after the fact that they are expected to gather evidence of student learning and other program performance, they often react with great resistance. If faculty and administrative position descriptions included the expectation of such evaluation skills and behavior, they could possibly make many improvements immediately, and improvements in the programs that prepare those faculty and administrators for service in higher education could be made as well.

Criteria for performance evaluation of faculty and administrators hired with the expectation that they will engage in outcomes-based assessment program review could include the extent to which the program evaluation was completed and the level of quality at which it was completed. Thus, rather than using program evaluation results for personnel evaluation, the focus would be on the quality practice of program evaluation and on opportunities for further professional development.

11. Possibly the most challenging aspect of all is preparing students for the higher education experience. While series of inputs assessments

can help institutions better understand the cognitive and noncognitive preparation of high school graduates, getting the students to graduate who represent the face of the nation continues to be a major challenge. Further, preparing all students for the type of learning that most faculty would like for them to experience also poses a challenge. Higher education institutions can't afford to ignore what is happening in K–12 education. We need to extend outreach in order to address these pipeline issues if we are serious about improving student learning and development.

While there are many other concerns about and possibilities for transformation that should take place, implementation of meaningful and manageable outcomes-based assessment program review can help to transform higher education. You can identify and improve quality in every aspect in the here and now. All you have to do is implement it in an effective, efficient, and enduring manner that respects your institutional culture.

GENERAL DESCRIPTIONS OF EACH GOOD PRACTICE INSTITUTION

Institution Name: Alverno College

Institution Size: 2,241
Institution Mission:

Alverno College is an institution of higher education dedicated to the undergraduate education of women. The student—her learning and her personal and professional development—is the central focus of everyone associated with Alverno. Alverno extends its mission of service and strengthens its ties to the community by offering graduate programs to both women and men. Agreement regarding this mission is evident throughout the college in its publications and operating philosophy. It is also the recurring theme in messages of the Board of Trustees and the president of the college, in catalogs and educational publications, and in the daily approach of faculty and staff to their work. The college's accomplishments are measured by how well we carry out this central mission.

Institution Website: http://www.alverno.edu

Institution Name: Azusa Pacific University

Institution Size: 8,218
Institution Mission:

"Azusa Pacific University is an evangelical Christian community of disciples and scholars who seek to advance the work of God in the world through academic excellence in liberal arts and professional programs of higher education that encourage students to develop a Christian perspective of truth and life.

Institution Websites: http://www.apu.edu; http://www.apu.edu/aima/

Institution Name: California State University at Monterey Bay

Institution Size: 3,760 (2003)
Institution Mission:

To build a multicultural learning community founded on academic excellence from which all partners in the educational process emerge prepared to contribute productively, responsibly, and ethically to California and the global community.

Institution Websites: http://csumb.edu/; http://iar.csumb.edu/

Institution Name: California State University at Sacramento

Institution Size: 27,972 (2004)
Institution Mission:

California State University, Sacramento, is an integral part of the community, committed to access, excellence and diversity.

California State University, Sacramento, is dedicated to the life-altering potential of learning that balances a liberal arts education with depth of knowledge in a discipline. We are committed to providing an excellent education to all eligible applicants who aspire to expand their knowledge and prepare themselves for meaningful lives, careers, and service to their community.

Reflecting the metropolitan character of the area, California State University, Sacramento, is a richly diverse community. As such, the university is committed to fostering in all its members a sense of inclusiveness, respect for human differences, and concern for others. In doing so, we strive to create a pluralistic community in which members participate collaboratively in all aspects of university life.

California State University, Sacramento, is committed to teaching and learning as its primary responsibility. In both the academic and student support programs, success is measured in terms of student learning. In addition, the university recognizes the vital connections among pedagogy and learning, research activities and classroom instruction, and co-curricular involvement and civic responsibility. All students, regardless of their entering levels of preparation, are expected to complete their degree programs with the analytical skills necessary to understand the social, economic, political, cultural, and ecological complexities of an increasingly interconnected world.

Institution Websites: http://www.csus.edu; http://www.oir.csus.edu/Reports/

Institution Name: Hampden-Sydney College

Institution Size: 1,082
Institution Mission:

Hampden-Sydney's first president, Samuel Stanhope Smith, described the mission of the college as the formation of good men and good citizens in an atmosphere of sound learning. In pursuit of this mission, Hampden-Sydney aims, through a comprehensive study of the liberal arts, to instill in selected students of ability a commitment to excellence and sound scholarship; to cultivate qualities of character rooted in ethical and religious values; to engender clear thinking and expression; to develop a broad understanding of the world and our place in it; to impart a comprehension of social institutions as a basis for the exercise of intelligent citizenship and community leadership; to prepare those with special interests and capacities for graduate study and research; and to equip graduates with the fundamental skills for a rewarding and productive life.

Institution Website: http://www.hsc.edu

Institution Name: Indiana University–Purdue University at Indianapolis (IUPUI)

Institution Size: 29,000
Institution Mission:
   To provide for its constituents excellence in:

- Teaching and Learning
- Research, Scholarship, and Creative Activity
- Civic Engagement, Locally, Nationally, and Globally

With each of these core activities characterized by:

- Collaboration within and across disciplines and with the community,
- A commitment to ensuring diversity, and
- Pursuit of best practices

IUPUI's mission is derived from and aligned with the principal components—Communities of Learning, Responsibilities of Excellence, Accountability and Best Practices—of Indiana University's Strategic Directions Charter.

Institution Website: http://www.iupui.edu

Institution Name: Isothermal Community College

Institution Size: 2,218
Institution Mission:
   Isothermal Community College exists to improve life through learning. In improving life through learning, we embrace the following values:

- A commitment to excellence
- Nurturing an organizational climate of integrity, care, and respect for individuals
- Innovation, evaluation, and informed change
- Elimination of barriers to learning
- Self-directed learning and critical thinking
- The preservation and perpetuation of our diverse cultural heritage

Institution Website: http://www.isothermal.cc.nc.us

Institution Name: John Carroll University

Institution Size: 4,350
Institution Mission:
   John Carroll is a Catholic and Jesuit University dedicated to developing women and men with the knowledge and character to lead and to serve.
Institution Website: http://www.jcu.edu

Institution Name: Keystone College

Institution Size: 1,450
Institution Mission:
   Keystone College is a fully accredited, independent, private college committed to helping all students attain their full potential. To achieve this goal, Keystone provides excellent instruction, close student-faculty relationships, personal attention, and individualized support services. Keystone College received formal approval from the Pennsylvania Department of Education to begin offering baccalaureate degree programs in 1998.
Institution Website: http://www.keystone.edu

Institution Name: Maryland Community Colleges

Institution Mission:
   The Maryland Association of Community Colleges (MACC) was established in 1992 as an advocacy organization for Maryland's public community colleges. All sixteen of Maryland's public community colleges are members of MACC and support the association through an annual institutional dues assessment.
Institution Website: http://www.mdacc.org/index.htm
Student Affairs' Affinity Group Website: http://www.mdacc.org/aboutus/affinity_gd_student.htm

Institution Name: Miami University

Institution Size: 22,600
Institution Mission:
   The mission of Miami University is to preserve, add to, evaluate, and transmit the accumulated knowledge of the centuries; to develop critical thinking, extend the frontiers of knowledge, and serve society; and to provide an environment conducive to effective and inspired teaching and learning, promote professional development of faculty, and encourage scholarly research and creativity of faculty and students.

Institution Website: http://www.miami.muohio.edu

Institution Name: New Jersey City University

Institution Size: 9,361
Institution Mission:
   The mission of New Jersey City University is to provide a diverse population with access to an excellent university education and the support services necessary for success. The university is also committed to the improvement of the educational, intellectual, cultural, socioeconomic, and physical environment of the surrounding urban region. Through implementation of this mission, New Jersey City University will become the best urban university in the United States.

Institution Website: http://www.njcu.edu

Institution Name: North Carolina State University

Institution Size: 29,637
Institution Mission:
   The mission of North Carolina State University is to serve its students and the people of North Carolina as a doctoral/research-extensive, land-grant university. Through the active integration of teaching, research, extension, and engagement, North Carolina State University creates an innovative learning environment that stresses mastery of fundamentals, intellectual discipline, creativity, problem solving, and responsibility. Enhancing its historic strengths in agriculture, science, and engineering with a commitment to excellence in a comprehensive range of academic disciplines, North Carolina State University provides leadership for intellectual, cultural, social, economic, and technological development within the state, the nation, and the world.

Institution Website: http://www.ncsu.edu

Institution Name: Oregon State University

Institution Size: 18,979

Institution Mission:

Oregon State University aspires to stimulate a lasting attitude of inquiry, openness, and social responsibility. To meet these aspirations, we are committed to providing excellent academic programs, educational experiences, and creative scholarship.

Institution Website: http://oregonstate.edu/

Institution Name: Sinclair Community College

Institution Size: 24,000

Institution Mission:

We help individuals turn dreams into achievable goals through accessible, high-quality, affordable learning opportunities.

Institution Website: http://www.sinclair.edu

Institution Name: Texas A&M University

Institution Size: 44,435

Institution Mission:

Texas A&M University is dedicated to the discovery, development, communication, and application of knowledge in a wide range of academic and professional fields. Its mission of providing the highest-quality undergraduate and graduate programs is inseparable from its mission of developing new understandings through research and creativity. It prepares students to assume roles of leadership, responsibility, and service to society. Texas A&M assumes as its historic trust the maintenance of freedom of inquiry and an intellectual environment nurturing the human mind and spirit. It welcomes and seeks to serve persons of all racial, ethnic, and geographic groups, women and men alike, as it addresses the needs of an increasingly diverse population and a global economy. In the twenty-first century, Texas A&M University seeks to assume a place of preeminence among public universities while respecting its history and traditions.

Institution Website: http://www.tamu.edu

Institution Name: Truman State University

Institution Size: 5,970

Institution Mission:

Truman State University is committed to the advancement of knowledge, to freedom of thought and inquiry, and to the personal, social, and intellectual growth of its students. The University strives to identify and maintain a recognized standard of excellence in all of its educational activities. The mission of Truman State University is to offer an exemplary undergraduate education to well-prepared students, grounded in the liberal arts and sciences, in the context of a public institution of higher education. To that end, the university offers affordable undergraduate studies in the traditional arts and sciences as well as selected preprofessional, professional, and master's-level programs that grow naturally out of the philosophy, values, content, and desired outcomes of a liberal arts education.

Institution Website: http://www.truman.edu

Institution Name: United States Naval Academy

Institution Size: 4,349
Institution Mission:
   To develop midshipmen morally, mentally and physically and to imbue them with the highest ideals of duty, honor and loyalty in order to provide graduates who are dedicated to a career of naval service and have potential for future development in mind and character to assume the highest responsibilities of command, citizenship and government.

Institution Website: http://www.usna.edu

Institution Name: University of Wisconsin at Whitewater

Institution Size: 10,540
Institution Mission:
   In addition to the system and core missions, the University of Wisconsin-Whitewater has the select mission to:

1. Offer an extensive range of undergraduate programs and degrees, including interdisciplinary programs in letters, sciences, and the arts, as well as programs and degrees leading to professional specialization.
2. Offer graduate education built clearly on its undergraduate emphases and strengths, with particular emphasis in business and education.
3. Expect scholarly activity, including research, scholarship, and creative endeavor, that supports its programs at the associate and baccalaureate degree level, its selected graduate programs, and its special mission.
4. Provide supportive services and programs for students with disabilities.
5. Recruit minority and nontraditional students and provide support services and programs for them.

6. Serve as a regional cultural and resource center.

7. Provide continuing education and outreach programs as an integrated institutional activity.

Institution Website: http://www.uww.edu

DEFINITIONS OF OUTCOMES-BASED ASSESSMENT

The following are definitions of outcomes-based assessment and outcomes-based assessment program review. In each case, where possible, the URL for the definition is listed so the reader can check for any updates since publication of this book. Many institutions update their own outcomes-based assessment program review materials as they learn through practice how to improve the process.

Alverno College

http://www.alverno.edu

John Carroll University

Submitted by Dr. Megan Moore Gardner

Assessment in student affairs yields information about the quality and utility of programs and services; enhances holistic student learning and development; informs practice and contributes to more intentional co-curricular learning opportunities for students; and encourages collaboration focused on student learning. The Division of Student Affairs uses a versatile assessment program that integrates the university mission, divisional strategic plan, divisional learning outcomes, departmental assessment plans, national and local surveys, the University Assessment Committee, the Student Affairs Assessment Team, and other assessment resources and tools. This multifaceted approach contributes to a comprehensive body of knowledge that informs planning and programming. The Division of Student Affairs views outcomes assessment as one piece of a larger assessment program that combines both student and academic affairs assessment to yield overall university outcomes. This is illustrated in the figure on page 160.

Sinclair Community College

http://www.sinclair.edu/about/assessment/principles/index.cfm
    Definition of Assessment: "a mindset that asks questions—good questions, hard questions, legitimate questions—about what and how much students are learning."
    —*Russell Edgerton*

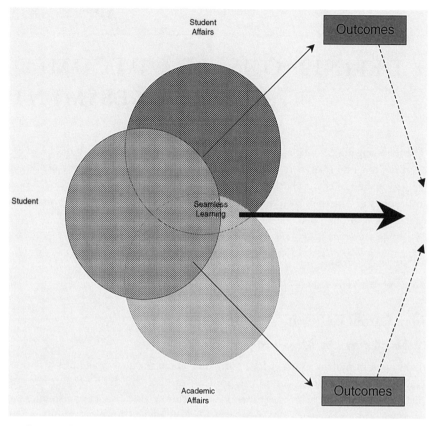

John Carroll University. Outcomes assessment as part of a larger assessment program.

CONCEPTUAL FRAMEWORKS FOR OUTCOMES-BASED ASSESSMENT PROGRAM REVIEW

The following are conceptual frameworks or guiding principles for outcomes-based assessment and outcomes-based assessment program review. In each case, where possible, the URL for the conceptual framework is listed so readers can check for any updates since publication of this book. Many institutions update their own outcomes-based assessment program review materials as they learn through practice how to improve the process.

Alverno College

Submitted by Marcia Mentkowski

We conceptualize inquiry to mean standing in, standing beside, and standing aside and sometimes to do all three simultaneously. We use the term *stand* here to give an active tone to a reflective activity that seeks continuous and expanded benefits for students: from the immediacy of the course-based experience of teaching and learning, to the collaborative and formative dimensions of activities for course and program development, to stepping away from the delivery of program or curriculum to take a summative, evaluative approach.

. . . For *Constructing* an Institutional and Program Assessment *Context*

1. Make a long-term commitment to a dynamic plan.
2. Rely on faculty questions for direction.
3. Create interactive processes.

. . . For *Designing and Doing* Institutional and Program Assessment

4. Define outcomes, criteria, and comparisons publicly.
5. Connect to student assessment.
6. Create public dialogue in a community of learning and judgment.

John Carroll University

Submitted by Megan Moore Gardner

The Division of Student Affairs uses a cyclical assessment process (see the figure that follows) that reviews programmatic, service, and student learning outcomes. It is informed by the mission, goals, and Jesuit, Catholic identity of the institution.

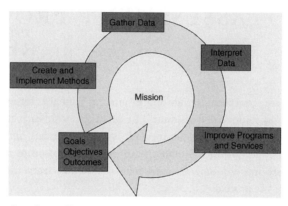

The Division of Student Affairs at Jonn Carroll University is immersed in assessment of programming, service, and student learning outcomes. Results of such efforts are used to improve programs and services and to enhance the overall student experience. The multifaceted approach results in a comprehensive body of knowledge about student learning, program quality, and services. Collaboration among student and academic affairs professionals contributes to overall institutional change and quality improvement.

Conceptual Understanding of Undergraduate Academic Program Review at North Carolina State University

http://www.NorthCarolinaStateUniversity.edu/provost/academic_programs/uapr/process/concept.html

Texas A&M University

http://assessment.tamu.edu/Conceptual%20Framework%20for%20EBDM.pdf

United States Naval Academy

Cited in Maki, 2004, p. 174–175.

COMMON OPERATIONAL LANGUAGE FOR OUTCOMES-BASED ASSESSMENT

The following are common operational language references for outcomes-based assessment and outcomes-based assessment program review. In each case, the URL for the document is listed so readers can check for any updates since publication of this book. Many institutions update their own outcomes-based assessment program review materials as they learn through practice how to improve the process.

North Carolina State University

http://www.NorthCarolinaStateUniversity.edu/provost/academic_programs/uapr/process/language.html

Sinclair Community College

Links to James Madison University—search program with definitions on assessment terms
http://people.jmu.edu/yangsx/

Texas A&M University

http://assessment.tamu.edu/Common%20Language%20for%20EBDM.pdf

OUTCOMES-BASED ASSESSMENT PROGRAM REVIEW GUIDELINES

The following are guidelines for outcomes-based assessment and outcomes-based assessment program review. In each case, the URL for the guideline is listed so readers can check for any updates made since publication of this book. Many institutions update their own outcomes-based assessment program review materials as they learn through practice how to improve the process.

Indiana University–Purdue University Indianapolis

http://www.planning.IndianaUniversity-PurdueUniversity-Indianapolis.edu/programre
view/IndianaUniversity-PurdueUniversity-Indianapolisprogramreview.html

North Carolina State University

Guidelines to Follow for Preparing Your Undergraduate Portfolio

http://www.NorthCarolinaStateUniversity.edu/provost/academic_programs/uapr/pro
cess/pre_2005_guidelines.htm

Guidelines for the Graduate Portfolio

http://www.fis.ncsu.edu/grad%5Fpublicns/program%5Freview/SS_Format1005.pdf

California State University at Monterey Bay

http://policy.csumb.edu/policies/approved_policies/program_review_model/index
.html

OUTCOMES-BASED ASSESSMENT PROGRAM REVIEW EXAMPLE TEMPLATES

Oregon State University
Division of Student Affairs
Services for Students with Disabilities
ASSESSMENT PLAN
FY 2004–2005

Date: January 14, 2004
Department: Services for Students with Disabilities
Director: Tracy Bentley-Townlin, Ph.D.
Assessment Contact: Jo Frederic
E-mail: Jo.D.Frederic@oregonstate.edu

Statement of Mission

The Office of Services for Students with Disabilities (SSD) facilitates the continued success of students with disabilities and the Oregon State University community by providing and promoting a supportive, accessible, and nondiscriminatory learning and working environment.

Statement of Goals

1. Provide effective accommodations for disabilities based on law and/or current best practices.
2. Educate the campus community about disability issues.
3. Positively influence decision making and practices to include universal design principles.
4. Promote self-determination for individuals with disabilities.

Statement of Outcomes

Goal 1: *Provide effective accommodations based on law and current best practices.*

Outcomes: *(SSD employees)*

A. *Student workers* will be able to navigate and demonstrate use of the online database, in the areas defined by the skills rubric, to assist SSD students who require additional assistance in requesting, monitoring, and updating their accommodations.

B. *Sign language interpreters* will demonstrate effective interpreting skills as defined by law and current best practices.

C. *Real-time transcribers* will demonstrate effective transcribing skills as defined by law and current best practices.

D. *Note takers and proctors* will demonstrate skills as defined by current best practices.

E. *Readers*

Outcomes: *(SSD students)*

F. *Students* will rate their accommodations an average of 4 ("very good") on a 5-point scale.

Goal 2: *Educate the campus community about disability issues.*

Outcomes: *(OSU faculty/staff)*

A. The number of requests for captioned videos SSD receives during 2004–05 with less than 48 hours' advance notice will decrease from FY 2003–2004 requests. Success if there is a 10 percent decline in requests with less than 48 hours.

B. The "Opportunity to Request Accommodations" statement will be provided on 70 percent or more of electronic notices for OSU events that are open to students and/or the public.

Outcomes: *(SSD employees)*

C. *Note takers* will complete the online note taker training and demonstrate knowledge about the deaf and hard of hearing community.

Goal 3: *Positively influence decision making to include universal design principles.*

Outcomes:

A. *Faculty* will report an increased knowledge of universal design and universal design for instruction (UD/UDI) principles as a result of participating in workshops on those topics during FY 2004–2005.

B. *Faculty* will apply UD/UDI principles in designing their courses.

Goal 4: *Promote and facilitate self-determination for individuals with disabilities.*

Outcomes:

A. *SSD students* will manage their accommodations by using the SSD online system to request, monitor, and update their requests for accommodations.

B. *SSD students* will submit requests for accommodations in a timely manner, using the SSD online system.

C. *SSD students* will be able to articulate the specific accommodations for which they are eligible and require for their success in the classroom and future endeavors.

Evaluation Methods

Goal 1: *Arrange effective accommodations based on law and current best practices.*

Outcomes:

A. *(SSD Student Employees):* The Administrative Assistant is developing a rubric to rate student employees' competency in use of the database. The students will be required to demonstrate and explain use of the database to the Administrative Assistant.

B. *(Interpreters):* In-class observations and evaluations by DHOH Coordinator. Evidence of RID certification. Student Satisfaction Survey: Interpreter; informal student interviews. Success if the students rate the interpreter at 3.5 or better on a 5-point scale in the Student Satisfaction Survey: Interpreter *and* if the Coordinator rates the interpreters 3.0 or better on a 5-point scale on performance evaluations of expressive and/or receptive interpreting and/or transliterating.

C. *(Transcribers):* Independent coding system. Evidence of certification. In-class observations and evaluations by DHOH coordinator. Success if transcribers meet the criteria for in-class transcribing and professional requirements.

D. *(Note takers and Proctors):* Survey; document informal interview, e-mail, and telephone comments. Review of note takers' notes for legibility, clarity, and completeness.

E. *(Readers)*

F. *(SSD Students):* Survey; document informal interview, e-mail, and telephone comments from students.

Goal 2: *Educate the campus community about disability issues.*

Outcomes:

A. Monitor the timeliness of requests from faculty for captioned videos. Count number of requests with less than 48 hours' advance notice; compare with data from FY 2003–2004.

B. Monitor and count the number of *OSU Today* e-mails that announce university or public events and include the "Opportunity to Request Accommodations" statement. Needs survey 2004–05.

C. Note taker completion of online training module; certificate of completion.

Goal 3: *Positively influence decision making to include universal design principles.*

Outcomes:

A. Survey of faculty members who attended the universal design workshops during FY 2004–05. Document interviews, e-mail, and phone comments of participants in the workshops.

B. Interviews; follow-up survey of faculty who attended the universal design workshops during FY 2004–05. Document UD/UDI principles that have been implemented in course planning. Document faculty report of reasons for failure to do so.

Goal 4: *Promote and facilitate empowerment and self-determination for individuals with disabilities.*

Outcomes:

A. Repeat administration of surveys related to the SSD online database given to students during Spring term 2004. Document student feedback (e-mail, interview, phone, etc.) Success if students rate use of the online database at 4 or above (5-point scale) on a satisfaction measurement instrument.

B. Count numbers of students eligible for priority registration. Success if 70 percent of students who qualify submit their schedules electronically within one week of date of priority registration.

2004–2005 Assessment Implementation

Goals	Outcomes	Method	Time	Who Responsible
Goal 1: Provide effective accommodations for disabilities based on law and/or current best practices.	A. *Student workers* will navigate and demonstrate use of the online database. *Revised 1/12/05	Hands-on skills test; observation and use of a "Skills Checklist" rubric. Success if students can perform 100% of the functions listed on the rubric *Revised 1/12/05	Over time 2004–06; as needed when new employees are hired	SSD Administrative Assistant
	B. *Interpreters* will demonstrate effective interpreting skills as defined by law and current best practices.	In-class observations; RID certification; performance evaluation; student interviews	Newly hired interpreters during year of hire 3-year evaluating/ reporting cycle to begin 2006–2007	Deaf/Hard of Hearing Access Services Coordinator
	C. *Transcribers* will demonstrate effective transcribing skills as defined by law and current best practices.	Independent coding system; Certification Level 1 and 2 exams; In-class observations	Newly hired transcribers during year of hire 3-year evaluating/ reporting cycle to begin 2006–2007	Deaf/Hard of Hearing (HOH) Access Services Coordinator
	D. *Note takers and proctors* will demonstrate effective note-taking and proctoring skills as defined by current best practices.	Survey; document informal interview, e-mail, and telephone comments; review of notes. Success if 70% of SSD students rate the service as "Good" or above on a 5-point scale	Spring Term 2005 3-year evaluating/ reporting cycle to begin 2006–2007	Alternative Testing/Note-Taking Coordinator
	E. *SSD students* will have access to the accommodations request system 24 hours/day by using the SSD online database.	Survey; document informal interview, e-mail, and telephone comments. Success if 80% of students rate the online system as "Good" or above on a rating scale and/or the majority of comments received are positive	Over time 2004–2007 3-year evaluating/ reporting cycle to begin 2006–2007	SSD Program Coordinators
Goal 2: Educate the campus community about disability issues.	A. Requests for captioned videos with less than 48 hours' advance notice will decrease from 2003–04 requests.	Count number of video requests received with less than 24 hours' advance notice; compare with 2003–04 data	2004–2005	Deaf/HOH Access Services Coordinator
	B. "Accommodations statement" will be provided on 30% or more of electronic notices for OSU events that are open to students and/or the public.	Monitor and document number of campus e-mails that carry the statement, compared with the total reviewed	Over time 2004–2007	Deaf/HOH Access Services Coordinator
	C. *Note takers* will complete the online training and demonstrate knowledge	Online training module. Success if 15% of note takers complete the online note-taker	FY 2004–2005	Alternative Testing/Note-Taking Coordinator

	about the deaf and hard of hearing community.	training and return the completed certificate to SSD.		
Goal 3: Positively influence decision making and practice to include universal design principles.	**A.** *Faculty* will report an increased knowledge of UD and UDI principles as a result of participation in workshops on those topics during FY 04-05.	Survey; informal interview, e-mail, and phone comments from faculty who attended the workshops. Success if 70% of participants report an increased knowledge of UDI as a result of the workshops	Over time 2004–2005	Director, Services for Students with Disabilities
	B. *Faculty* will include UD/UDI principles in course design.	Survey; interviews (e-mail, telephone, in-person)	Over time 2005–2008 Assessment/reporting of results 2007–2008	Director, Services for Students with Disabilities
Goal 4: Promote self-determination for individuals with disabilities.	**A.** *SSD students* will have access to the accommodations request system 24 hours/day by using the SSD online database. Students will manage their accommodations by requesting, monitoring, and updating their requests for accommodations by using the SSD online system.	Tracking numbers of students who use database. Counting numbers of students who participate in database training sessions. Student interviews. Counting numbers of students who require additional one-on-one assistance. Student satisfaction surveys. Success if 70% of students rate themselves as comfortable using the online system	Over time 2004–2007 Assessment/reporting of results 2006–07	SSD Program Coordinators
	B. *SSD students* will submit their requests for accommodations in a timely manner, using the SSD online system.	Counting numbers of students who are eligible for priority registration. Success if 80% of students who qualify for priority registration submit their requests electronically within one week of the date of priority registration	Over time 2004–2007 Assessment/reporting of results 2006–07	SSD Program Coordinators

North Carolina State University
Department of History
B.A. and B.S. in History
PROGRAM REVIEW
Submitted by Mike Carter

Program Objectives

The objectives of the faculty of the Department of History are to:

1. encourage its majors to develop historical awareness, perspective, and understanding;
2. provide instruction and guidance to enable majors to apply sound historical research skills; and
3. help its majors to understand the standard forms of historical expression, to critique historical arguments made by others, and to produce historical arguments themselves.

Program Outcomes

1. *Historical Awareness, Perspective, and Understanding*

Graduates of the history program should be able to appreciate the varieties of cultural experience in history. Specifically, graduates should demonstrate that they:

a. have acquired a basic knowledge of the changing traditions and values that have operated in western culture;
b. have acquired a basic knowledge of the changing traditions and values that have operated in non-western or pre-modern societies;
c. can explain the historical development of events, institutions, and social values;
d. can pose historical questions about the problems that run through human history and about historical continuities and discontinuities; and
e. can show how the past is connected to the present by applying a critical perspective to their own place in history.

2. *Historical Research Skills*

Graduates of the history program should understand the nature of historical interpretation, the variety of historical sources, and the structure of historical argument and be able to apply that understanding to answering historical questions. Specifically, graduates should demonstrate that they can:

a. pose a significant research question about history;
b. locate relevant primary and secondary sources for investigating a research question;
c. critically evaluate primary and secondary sources in terms of credibility, authenticity, interpretive stance, audience, potential biases, and value for answering the research question;
d. interpret the sources fairly and accurately in an answer to a research question; and
e. marshal the evidence from the research to support a historical argument for an answer to a research question.

3. *Historical Expression*

Graduates of the history program should be able to demonstrate that they are informed and critical consumers and producers of history. Specifically, graduates should demonstrate that they:

a. can apply a critical perspective to evaluating historical arguments, including the quality of the sources, the validity of the interpretations of those sources, and the soundness of the argument's use of evidence to support a historical interpretation, and
b. have mastered the oral and written forms of communication appropriate to history, such as the critical book review, summary of readings, critical discussion of an argument, historical narrative based on sources, and research paper.

Sources of Data for Assessing Program Outcomes

Portfolios of student work should include:

- written reflections on their awareness of their place in history (written in response to their experience doing the research paper they will turn in for outcome 2), and
- a research paper from a 400-level course that the student chooses as the best representation of his or her research skills.

Students' Academic Degree Audits (ADAs; should exhibit sufficient depth of academic study in western culture)
Senior exit interviews

Faculty surveys
Student Research Skills Survey to be given in 491

Outcome 1: *Historical Awareness, Perspective, and Understanding*

Graduates' ability to appreciate the varieties of cultural experience in history

1a. to acquire a basic knowledge of the changing traditions and values that have operated in western culture

- Students' ADAs (should exhibit sufficient depth of academic study in western culture)
- Senior exit interviews

1b. to acquire a basic knowledge of the changing traditions and values that have operated in non-Western or pre-modern societies

- Students' ADAs (should exhibit sufficient diversity of academic study of non-western and pre-modern societies)
- Senior exit interviews

1c. to explain the historical development of events, institutions, and social values

- Faculty survey of 491 teachers

1d. to pose historical questions about the problems that run through human history and about historical continuities and discontinuities

- Faculty survey of 491 teachers

1e. to show how the past is connected to the present by applying a critical perspective to their own place in history

- Faculty survey of 491 teachers
- Portfolio of student work: written reflections on their awareness of their place in history (written in response to their experience doing the research paper they will turn in for outcome 2)

Outcome 2: *Historical Research Skills*

Graduates' ability to understand the nature of historical interpretation, the variety of historical sources, and the structure of historical argument and be able to apply that understanding to answering historical questions

- Portfolio of student work: research paper from a 400-level course that the student chooses as the best representation of his or her research skills
- Student Research Skills Survey to be given in 491
- Faculty survey

Outcome 3. *Historical Expression*

Graduates' ability to demonstrate that they are informed and critical consumers and producers of history

- Faculty survey
- Senior exit interview

Review Cycles

Initial Program Review Cycle

2001–2002:   Develop program objectives, outcomes, and assessment plan; initiate assessment of outcomes

August 2002: Preliminary program review report submitted to CHASS (College of Humanities, Arts & Social Sciences) Dean and to Committee for Undergraduate Program Review:

- program objectives
- program outcomes
- program review plan
- results of initial assessment
- description of assessment activities to be carried out in the following year

Fall 2002:   Continue gathering assessment data and complete assessment of outcomes

Spring 2003: Assessment reports submitted to departmental Curriculum Committee:

- description of process of assessing program outcomes
- results of assessment
- recommendations for changes in curriculum and/or changes in outcomes and assessment plan

Departmental Curriculum Committee considers recommendations and takes them to faculty for discussion and approval

August 2003: Full program review portfolio completed and submitted to college for review and then, with any necessary revisions, to Committee for Undergraduate Program Review

Subsequent Seven-Year Cycles for University Program Review

2003–2006: Continue gathering assessment data at appropriate intervals

Fall 2005: Complete assessment of outcomes; assessment reports (including description of assessment process, results, and recommendations for changes in curriculum and changes in outcomes and assessment plan) submitted to Curriculum Committee

Spring 2006: Curriculum Committee considers recommendations and takes them to faculty for discussion and approval

August 2006: Full program review portfolio completed and submitted to college for review and then, with any necessary revisions, to Committee for Undergraduate Program Review

2006–2010: Etc.

Truman State University

See http://assessment.truman.edu

HAMPDEN-SYDNEY COLLEGE PRIMARY TRAIT ANALYSIS OF RHETORIC 102 PORTFOLIOS

Assessment Scale

4 = Strong degree of control
3 = Reasonable control
2 = Inconsistent control
1 = Poor control

Domains and Features

- Clarity/quality of idea/thinking/thesis, all ideas in essays
  — Significance
  — Depth
  — Complexity
  — Originality
  — Unified sense of purpose

- Use of evidence/development/coherence/reasoning/organization
  — Paragraphing
  — Accuracy in use of evidence (quoted correctly)
  — Appropriateness
  — Variety

- Rhetorical Style
  — Conciseness
  — Effective sentences
  — Emphasis
  — Variety
  — Parallelism
  — Tact/gracefulness in incorporating quotations

- Mastery of usage/grammar/correctness
  - — Mastery of conventions (documentation)
  - — (Wordiness)
  - — (Parallelism)

Draft composed at staff workshop, April 15, 2000

HAMPDEN-SYDNEY COLLEGE RHETORIC PROFICIENCY EXAM PRIMARY TRAIT ANALYSIS SCORING GUIDE

Essay number: _____

Please circle all the descriptors below that best describe the essay:

Presence of a Thesis

1. The thesis is stated clearly and is worded effectively.
2. It is clear what the thesis is from the introduction, but it is not worded especially well.
3. The essay's thesis is not clearly stated in the introduction but becomes evident as the essay develops.
4. It is unclear what the thesis is—the essay doesn't seem to have a central point.

Quality of the Thesis

5. The thesis is valid, original, and provocative, suggesting a complex idea.
6. The thesis is valid if mundane or not very original or complex. But it nonetheless suggests a serviceable central point and illustrates that the writer understands the concept of establishing a debatable assertion.
7. The thesis lacks depth or complexity to the extent that the argument cannot be convincing because the initial idea is so limited.
8. The thesis relies on the language of the question without moving beyond its terms, without suggesting that the writer will establish his own argument.
9. The thesis is untenable and cannot be supported.

Organization and Development of Ideas

10. The support for the thesis is strong at all levels: there is sufficient evidence and detail; the reasoning is clear; and the ideas are well-organized, both within individual paragraphs and as the writer moves from paragraph to paragraph.

11. The thesis is adequately supported by detailed evidence and logical reasoning; some portions may be less well developed, less well organized, or less clear than others, but overall, the writer presents convincing evidence in a convincing fashion.

12. The support for the thesis is not adequate to make the case convincing because:

    a. The support for the case repeats rather than develops ideas/there is inadequate development to fully support the thesis; assertions are not supported with evidence and reasons.

    b. How the evidence supports the thesis is unclear, or parts of the argument are unclear enough that they render the logic of the essay confusing.

    c. The evidence, while it may seem detailed enough and valid, is poorly organized, giving an impression of random presentation of ideas.

    d. The evidence for the central assertion relies heavily on material in the published essay and doesn't show original thinking or provide fresh examples.

13. The essay is organized according to the five-paragraph essay formula or some other very formulaic structure.

Grammar, Style, and Diction

14. The writer of the essay has excellent control over grammar and conventions of standard written English; the essay is virtually free from errors in mechanics and usage.

15. The writer of the essay is largely in control of grammar; the frequency and seriousness of errors do not significantly mar the essay.

16. The writer of the essay has inconsistent control over grammar, and frequent and or serious errors do interfere with the overall clarity of the essay.

17. The writer of the essay has very poor control over grammar, rendering the essay very difficult to read because of the number and/or types of mechanical errors.

18. The writer shows a strong degree of control over sentence structure, often using sophisticated structures and presenting ideas in a way that makes their expression interesting.

19. The writer shows some degree of control over sentence structure; the style, even if not especially sophisticated, is also not overly simplistic and leaves the impression of readability.

20. The writer frequently employs simple sentence structures, showing a lack of stylistic maturity in the writing. The essay may not read well or may leave the impression of choppiness because the style is so simplistic.

21. The writer shows inconsistent control over sentence structure; the ideas are sometimes hard to follow because of tangled syntax.

22. The writer shows very poor control over sentence structure; the ideas are frequently hard to follow, and the essay may seem virtually unreadable as a result of poor syntax.

23. The writer shows control over diction
    a. always—careful word choice enhances the essay's presentation of ideas.
    b. most of the time—a few inappropriate word choices don't mar the essay significantly.
    c. sometimes—but inexact word choices do detract from the essay's impact.
    d. rarely—frequent instances of poor word choice interfere with meaning.

Comments: (please provide brief comments if you wish)

MATRIX FOR ALIGNING ACCREDITATION WITH PROGRAM REVIEW DEADLINES

North Carolina State University

See http://www.ncsu.edu/undergrad_affairs/assessment/assess.htm

Texas A&M University

See http://assessment.tamu.edu

EXAMPLE OF A CONCEPT MAP

For an example of a concept map, see the Oregon State University's Master's in Student Affairs Curriculum Map at http://styluspub.com/resources/outcomes-basedprogramreview.aspx.

A DESCRIPTION OF ALVERNO COLLEGE'S OUTCOMES-BASED ASSESSMENT PROGRAM REVIEW

Learning-Centered Assessment at the Program Level: Exploring Principles, Guidelines, and Criteria through the Study of Practice at Alverno College

William H. Rickards, Glen Rogers, and Marcia Mentkowski
Alverno College

Program review can take various forms. For faculty members in a discipline department, it can be a means of exploring their practice or trying to understand the teaching that supports their students' learning most effectively. In these cases, program review is much like the self-assessments that students perform to understand and consolidate their own learning. In other cases, it can serve administrative functions that aid in planning and decision making. However, in practice, program review as a management tool can trump its reflective and investigative dimensions. We are using the term *program assessment* here to cover activities that might include program review, a department's evaluation of student learning outcomes, and its use of findings for curriculum improvement. In the case of Alverno College, practices of program and institutional assessment integrate roles of inquiry, improving instruction, curriculum evaluation, and institution-wide accountability for maximizing both learning outcomes and resources.

Our intent in this chapter is to explore a set of practices at the program level in the context of the development of an integrated system of student, program, and institutional assessment. The approach and examples we include stress the college's underlying commitment to improving educational practice and providing for institutional review of programs. As contributors to this book of practices in outcomes assessment, our intent is, first, to describe the foundations of program-level assessment as it emerged from student assessment and its learning principles. Second, we set forth defining elements from the Student Learning Initiative (Doherty, Riordan, & Roth, 2002) for program, curriculum, and institution-wide assessment to address adaptability of practices across learning-centered institutions. Third, we offer a set of guidelines for implementation and explore these through a set of practice examples from different Alverno departments. Our goal is to articulate the fundamentals of our practice for peer debate and discussion.

Foundations of Program and Institutional Assessment in Individual Student Assessment

The development of educational practice at Alverno College is centered primarily on student learning. Over time, program assessment has emerged, alongside student assessment, as a key component of a learning-centered institution (Mentkowski & Loacker, 1985). Assessment practices were based first on faculty concern for individual student learning and then developed further through studying student learning, faculty teaching, and student assessment itself. Alverno faculty call this assessment focus on individual student learning *student assessment-as-learning.* They define it as a multidimensional process that is integral to learning and involves observation and judgment of each student's performance on the basis of explicit criteria, with feedback to the student for improving learning and to the faculty for improving teaching. It certifies student achievement in developing academic knowledge and abilities required for graduation (Alverno College Faculty, 1994).

From this perspective, an assessment system that makes a critical contribution to an educational program's transformation actually begins with faculty's conversations and reflections on learning and teaching (Loacker & Mentkowski, 1993; Mentkowski, 1998). Such conversations naturally lead to questions about what is learned and how it happens, as content outcomes in disciplines and professions and as generic abilities that transfer across domains (see Maki, 2004).

For Alverno, the integration of content and abilities in the early 1970s led to an ability-based curriculum that supports teaching toward student learning outcomes. Faculty members decided that students would be required to develop and demonstrate a set of generic abilities so they could integrate and transfer learning over multiple contexts—and as a result set the stage for developing a new curriculum theory (see Riordan & Roth, 2005). And so, in courses and assessments across the curriculum, faculty specified learning outcomes and developmental criteria for learning and performance in a discipline or profession for integrating content and these abilities.[1] As Alverno educators formulated *learning principles,* they connected these

---

[1] The abilities were initially articulated in 1973 and have been refined constantly over time. They are, currently, analysis, communication, problem solving, social interaction, valuing in decision making, effective citizenship, developing a global perspective, and aesthetic engagement.

to *design principles for student assessment.* For example, the first two immediate connections are (a) if learning that lasts is active and independent, integrative and experiential, assessment must judge performance in contexts related to life roles, and (b) if learning that lasts is self-aware, reflective, self-assessed, and self-regarding, assessment must include explicitness of expected outcomes, public criteria, and student self-assessment (Alverno College Faculty, 1994; Mentkowski & Associates, 2000). Here Alverno faculty were realizing in their discourse how assessments that elicited the depth of performances that would allow them to judge student progress would also aid students in constructing their learning.

These commitments to the learning of each student also led Alverno to design assessments to support the review and development of programs, departments, and the college's institution-wide curriculum. At these levels, the assessment efforts integrated the perspectives of the educators themselves—faculty, academic staff, and educational researchers—as a community of learners whose members were constantly trying to make their practices more effective.

Over time, Alverno scholarship on connecting learning theory to assessment design grounded an integrated assessment system in articulated learning principles. Three additional learning principles articulated by Alverno faculty suggest connections between student and program-level assessment: (c) if learning that lasts is developmental and individual, assessment must include multiplicity and be cumulative and expansive; (d) if learning that lasts is interactive and collaborative, assessment must include feedback and external perspectives as well as performance; and (e) if learning that lasts is situated and transferable, assessment must be multiple in mode and context (Alverno College Faculty, 1994; Mentkowski & Associates, 2000).

Thus, the assessment system can operate at multiple levels—individual, course, program, and institution—and still provide for the coherence necessary for a multidisciplinary practice of institution-wide assessment. The multiple-level assessment system is primarily characterized by longitudinal studies of the effects of Alverno's primary educational practices during and after college for studying the validity of its emerging curriculum theory: Students integrate and transfer learning from an integrated liberal arts and professions curriculum, across courses and over time (see Mentkowski & Associates, 2000.). Institutional assessment also included the study of assessment instruments and allowed for validating the student assessment system as a whole.

As these broader results became available, faculty members were also focusing attention at the department level. Program reviews occasionally were carried out as descriptive, administrative tasks, based largely on enrollment, number of graduates, curriculum design, and course requirements and usually conducted under the structure of the college curriculum committee. But when the focus was on the student learning outcomes of a specialized curriculum in a discipline or professional department, departments have increasingly collaborated with the college's educational research and evaluation department in a process structured as an *evaluation of the major field.* This process supports a department's evidence-based judgments about values, worth, and effectiveness of the major for student and alumna learning. Program assessment processes developed quickly in undergraduate professional programs like nursing and teacher education, partially in response to specialized accreditation agencies.

Standing Aside from the Alverno Difference

Now we stand aside from the Alverno experience and ask how different institutions might learn from a program assessment practice that has evolved in its own unique way. The college's research focus on student learning and curriculum and its participation in various consortia have presented major opportunities to study our practices in relation to others, including those that deal with program and institutional levels of assessment. Together, these consortia have given us some sense of what may generalize across practices (Mentkowski, in press; Mentkowski & Loacker, 2002).

Program Assessment Elements

We also recognize that educational practices are shaped by context. For us, what seems to matter as we have worked with smaller and larger institutions across consortia is size and scale of an institution.[2] Degree of focus on teaching also makes a difference (Alverno's primary mission is teaching for student learning). We have found that some particular strategies and structures that we implement do not necessarily transfer to other campuses; similarly, policies that may seem effective or necessary in a specific context—like the large scale of a comprehensive university or state higher education system—may not readily serve the needs of a small college or even a department within a larger institution. However, Alverno's underlying learning principles shape common elements that may have considerable meaning across different educational settings, in contrast to Alverno's underlying curriculum theory about what students should study and need to demonstrate for graduation (Riordan & Roth, 2005).

To illustrate, Alverno joins the Student Learning Initiative (Doherty, Riordan, & Roth, 2002) in defining program assessment less in terms of formal procedures and

---

[2] As of fall 2004, Alverno has 102 full-time and 116 part-time faculty members and a heterogeneous student body of 2,241 from a wide range of ethnicities, family backgrounds, and academic preparation. Most live off-campus in the city and surrounding metropolitan area. Alverno was chartered as a college for women and has a relatively recent graduate program that is co-ed.

required elements and more in terms of elements or descriptive criteria that characterize the effective use of assessment to develop educational practice and its outcomes in student learning. We concur that, for learning-centered institutions, program, curriculum, and institution-wide assessment

- is integral to learning about student learning;
- creates processes that assist faculty, staff, and administrators to improve student learning;
- involves inquiry to judge program value and effectiveness for fostering student learning;
- generates multiple sources of feedback to faculty, staff, and administrators about patterns of student and alumni performance in relation to learning outcomes that are linked to curriculum;
- makes comparisons of student and alumni performance to standards, criteria, or indicators (faculty, disciplinary, professional, accrediting, certifying, legislative) to create public dialogue;
- yields evidence-based judgments of how students and alumni benefit from the curriculum, co-curriculum, and other learning contexts; and
- guides curricular, co-curricular, institution-wide improvements (Doherty, Riordan, & Roth, 2002, p. 22).

We now take a further look at program assessment through the lens of guidelines for implementation drawn from practice that may also operate across different educational contexts. Our hope is to add to the body of knowledge about program-level assessment as an emerging element in higher education scholarship. We ask:

- What are some broad guidelines and concerns drawn from Alverno's case that may be meaningful for learning-centered program assessment more generally?
- How are some of the implied commitments realized in our own practices?

Program Assessment Guidelines

An integrated review of the college's practices in working with assessment processes and student outcomes resulted in six guidelines for institutional assessment that could lead to educational coherence and improvement. These are summarized in figure 1.

The first two guidelines address the construction of the larger context in which institutional assessment proceeds and develops meaning.

1. Make a long-term commitment to a dynamic plan. This major step connects inquiry, educational planning, and the institution or program's sense of mission. It is

FIGURE 1
Six Guidelines for Constructing an Assessment Context

1. Make a long-term commitment to a dynamic plan.
2. Rely on faculty questions for direction.
3. Create interactive processes.
4. Define outcomes, criteria, and comparisons publicly.
5. Connect to student assessment.
6. Create public dialogue in a community of learning and judgment.

Adapted from Mentkowski, 1991/1994.

frequently a necessary step in planning for accreditation visits, but it may also involve modest—if persistent—steps in recurring planning. The intention is that program and institutional assessment be oriented toward a developing scholarship in support of the campus's service of students and their learning. A dynamic plan is critical so that the efforts have a foundation in the institution's commitments and do not simply react to external pressures (e.g., an upcoming accreditation visit).

2. Rely on faculty questions for direction. Anchoring the inquiry activities in the needs and interests of educators is critical to the integrated nature of the endeavor. What do faculty members want to know? What do departments want to know? What does the institution as a whole want to know? What do students want to know? What do external audiences want to know? These are the questions that frequently begin program inquiries, and we return to them with every new effort.

The next four guidelines deal with the design and conduct of institutional assessment.

3. Create interactive processes. The concern here is to provide structure that engages faculty and staff from across a program or institution in conversations that deepen their investment in the inquiry. We have found that involving interdisciplinary faculty and staff yields benefits throughout assessment inquiry—in interpreting assessment findings, drawing any implications, and participating in design for successive steps. These kinds of meetings and involvements typically require structure and planning to enable a depth of sustained involvement by a whole department, stakeholders from diverse academic units, and supporting staff.

4. Define outcomes, criteria, and comparisons publicly. Through the design and analytic stages of assessment activities, it is critical that the range of faculty and staff involved recognize and understand the plans. The structures and models of curriculum evaluation have varied over the last several years. Some have taken a form similar to that of the standardized tests of K–12 education (e.g., Steele, 1989; Steele &

Lutz, 1995). For example, teaching and nursing use state licensing exams that can measure program effectiveness, if only in terms of pass rates. But more often, evaluations consist of multiple data sources that are combined in integrated analysis and judgment (e.g., Haworth & Conrad, 1997; Zeichner, 2000).

As plans emerge, multiplicity of perspective and attention to externality are important considerations in creating designs and analytic comparisons. The role of externality is to examine findings from local activities against more broadly recognized standards or expectations. This helps educators to challenge their own assumptions and to build credibility of and confidence in analyses.

Although much is known or accepted as standard in higher education, there is a great deal that educators and researchers do not know and need to learn. In this context, some program studies need to be more descriptive and discovery-oriented, just as some need to use careful analysis of program effects. Understanding the uses of different study approaches and how to integrate them into a larger and sustained system of inquiry into student learning requires that programs have the resources and creativity to adjust methods as needed and implement with rigor.

Because of the complexity of most programs and the questions that emerge, various approaches to curriculum inquiry need to be considered. For example, the recent work on design-based studies—with the fluid introduction of teaching innovations in classroom contexts—has shown great promise for bringing rigor into instructional research and program assessments (Design-Based Research Collective, 2003). This work is particularly relevant when assessments to serve individual student learning are also designed to serve as evidence in program-level assessments. In practice, the inquiry builds on the existing assessment system and, specifically, on key performances from curriculum-embedded assessments (e.g., capstone course performances, portfolios, speeches, papers, logs, assessor checklists). When embedded assessments serve research purposes and program assessment needs, there may be other concerns, such as how to systematically collect and aggregate performance data. This is particularly the case where assessments are based on live unrecorded performance. In such instances, using qualitative and deliberative research methods may become even more important.

5. Connect to student assessment. Current assessment practices have opened a window into classroom practices, because program observations are being made through assessments embedded in everyday teaching and learning. In this context it is all the more important that abstractions about student learning—those that are generated out of multiple data sources—be presented in ways that link back to the performances faculty will likely see in their own practices. This has frequently meant that alongside sophisticated data analysis, faculty can be deeply engaged by seeing or reading student performances. Samples from embedded assessments have face validity and meaning, if only because they connect with the ways in which faculty generally experience students' work.

6. Create public dialogue in a community of learning and judgment. Public dialogue about student learning establishes a participatory framework in which educators can explore their diverse interests and shape their plans and interpretations. Our intent with this guideline is to recognize the role that dialogue plays in educational practice and anticipate the interactive, dialogic dimensions of the assessment processes. As work moves forward, it is important that it encourage educators to

- share discoveries about teaching and learning;
- make persuasive, evidence-based judgments so others can construct their own meaning about what works and what can make education better;
- create processes for linking insights with continuous improvement; and
- extend the conversation to various publics.

Teacher discourse plays a large role in educational practice. As noted in Mentkowski and Associates (2000, pp. 279–287), ideas about teaching and learning often move into educational practice through the reflective conversations of teachers. Therefore, it is critical that a program assessment also envision the kind of discussions that are warranted and support them through reporting and engagement in interpretive processes.

The traditional means of communicating review and evaluation activities has been a report or document, and these continue to serve important purposes as hard copy records. However, this guideline emphasizes the interactive, deliberative, and public nature of inquiries designed to support the continuing development of a campus or of support for faculty learning. Even reports can be constructed interactively so they integrate multiple viewpoints (e.g., through authorship that combines research, teaching, and practice perspectives). Additional reporting and documentation procedures may range from technical reports produced by research staff, to full assessment reports co-authored by faculty and research staff, to planning documents and minutes that are essentially faculty authored. (For additional considerations on evaluation reporting, see Torres, Preskill, & Piontek, 1996.)

Practice-Based Examples

In this section, we discuss examples from the philosophy and education departments. Each of these is designed to demonstrate an important process of faculty judging and improvising their department-level outcomes and to explore how the guidelines discussed above shape the conduct and design of program assessment.

Student Performance and Faculty Deliberation: Each department at Alverno has articulated learning outcomes that are distributed across courses and addressed through assessments. These assessments and student performance on them become an important part of faculty deliberations. This is both a discourse on student progress and an effort to coordinate activities among courses. In conversations about student performance and ongoing planning and collaboration, faculty draw on student performance as an evidentiary basis for considering the outcomes of the curriculum. For example, one of the philosophy student learning outcomes for the majors is "uses consistency and logic as tools in developing/following the arguments/perspectives of selected philosophers" (Alverno College Philosophy Faculty, 2003, p. 3). Faculty members had observed that while students in their courses were articulating the principles and directions of particular philosophical perspectives, they occasionally struggled to develop the complex line of reasoning in some perspectives. From these conversations, faculty members designed learning experiences throughout the course sequence so that students would pay more attention to developing arguments, both in analyzing those posed by philosophers and in refining their own ability to pose philosophical arguments (see Engelmann, 2005).

This example is drawn from the everyday conversations of faculty who are engaged in assessing their students' learning. While the faculty do not necessarily share the same courses, their common commitment to fundamental learning outcomes and their interactions become the basis for curriculum development. Faculty members are making comparisons between their extensive experience of course-based student performance and their expectations of student performance across a range of venues. At the same time, understanding how this discourse proceeds can become a critical part of assessment and evaluation activities at a department or program level. We have found ourselves asking particular kinds of questions to help understand how this discourse proceeds. What helps to structure and focus faculty members' observations? What kinds of data will help them reflect on teaching and learning? How does continuing study of student learning contribute to building policies and practices across various courses and teaching roles?

Faculty members monitor student progress through complex, multidimensional performances. The systematic review of a major field generally involves a synthesis or aggregation of complex, multidimensional performances triangulated with data from other sources, such as progress in the curriculum and persistence to graduation, student perspectives on their learning, and alumna evaluations. The nature and demands of these analytic comparisons often benefit from collaboration with resource persons outside the discipline or support department. At Alverno, the educational research and evaluation department has often served as a collaborative partner in program evaluation inquiries. This office has been particularly concerned with bringing review methods that could work with the complexity of the data, engage faculty members in analysis and interpretation, and operate efficiently within department resources. In these collaborative efforts, the individual departments remain leaders in conceiving and conducting program evaluation.

A Historical Perspective on Program Assessment and Development: Sustaining Inquiry: In the 1990s, the education department initiated an ongoing chronological documentation of changes in the curriculum in relation to sources of evidence that led to these changes. The recorded studies involved diverse research approaches (including graduate surveys, portfolio analysis, field observation, and faculty deliberation), but the chronology essentially presents functional descriptions of activities and their effects. For example, the department's documentation linked (a) its strengthening of the integration of technology across the curriculum to feedback from candidates and graduates as well as emerging standards in the professional associations; (b) increased attention to the range of student needs to a triangulated study of ratings of Alverno student teacher performance by cooperating teachers, supervising faculty, and the aspiring teachers themselves; and (c) revisions in field courses to self-ratings by teacher graduates from Alverno and other teacher education programs. The examples in the chronology of inquiry and change included collaborative studies with Educational Research and Evaluation as well as many evaluation activities conducted by the department alone.

We have found that documenting curriculum development and evidence sources in this chronology has a number of powerful benefits. It has provided affirmation across the department of the scope and nature of its evaluation activities. In addition, it has enabled the department to communicate its sustained commitment to program assessment to external audiences. It has helped sustain institutional memory and provide the basis for a historical analysis of key elements in inquiries across time. For example, we have described a textured picture of how the education program has used inquiry to guide curriculum planning (Rickards, Rogers, & Lake, 2004). In addition, because this process has obvious potential for positive bias, it was critical to account for the procedures in individual studies and to compare the perspectives of various members through targeted interviews.

Student Performance, Systematic Inquiry, and Program Assessment: Study of the portfolios created by teacher candidates has become an increasingly important source of information on progress of these future teachers. Part of the challenge here has been developing a systematic analysis that builds on the deliberative processes of the faculty. With sufficient attention to preparing the review process, departments have been able to complete a meaningful review of a representative set of complex multidimensional performance from a sample of portfolios in the context of a single meeting.

For example, in spring 2000, the Education and Educational Research and Evaluation departments collaborated in focusing on the teaching effectiveness project students completed as a student teaching portfolio in the final practicum. Thirteen education faculty members were able to review the student teaching portfolios of eleven teacher candidates in one eighty-minute segment of a faculty meeting. Educational research and evaluation researchers provided design assistance and support. The portfolio elements for each teacher candidate included background on her placement and students, lesson or unit plans with assessment strategies, an analysis of student learning, self-assessment of performance against state standards, and her reflection on her future growth as a teacher.

In the review, each of the participating faculty members received and rated three of the portfolio performances for whether it did not meet, met, exceeded, or was an outstanding example of meeting the standards for the various components. All members referred a single referent case, and two to three participants rated each of the remaining cases. The faculty members first read the portfolios separately, taking notes and making their judgments. Then they met in small groups to discuss common cases. Finally the faculty met as a whole to discuss the sample, anchoring their observations in the referent case.

The full department discussion reinforced faculty's shared standards for performance, while it also clarified the areas where the education faculty members had the most serious concerns about the performance of the teacher candidates in relation to state standards and department criteria. The department was concerned about the candidates' analysis of their students' learning, particularly in relation to their own teaching performance. Faculty members raised questions about what candidates were learning in their sequence of prior courses that would prepare them for this task, observing that the earlier performances seemed more solid than those in final field placement. However, they also recognized that those performances were supported by more context and structure. Subsequently, the department revised the activities in the field placements before student teaching, requesting that the candidates conduct more complex and independent analyses of the relationship between their teaching and their students' learning. (Note: Additional information on this activity and related commentary is available in Maki, 2004.)

Studying the Competence of Graduates: As a capstone performance in the curriculum, the teaching effectiveness project discussed above offers an opportunity to demonstrate the professional competence of graduating seniors from the teacher education program. A key aspect of the development of the teaching effectiveness project has involved coordinating the department's existing definition of required abilities for graduation with newly emerging professional standards for teacher performance articulated at state and national levels (e.g., National Council for Accreditation of Teacher Education, 2002). However, in the context of the department's specialized accreditation, aggregate summaries of teacher education performance are required.

As a method for producing meaningful, aggregate descriptions of performance, research staff thematically analyzed forty student teaching performances. This analysis focused on the candidates' lesson plans, assessment designs, how they analyzed their students' performances, and their self-assessments as developing teachers (Alverno College Office of Educational Research and Evaluation, 2000). Excerpted examples of student performance within the thematic categories enabled the research staff to illustrate teacher candidate performance on a number of analytical dimensions. As a complementary method of aggregation, the researchers focused more specifically on coding the students' narrative self-assessments of their performance against specified criteria. These criteria were based on both the curriculum-based framework for self-assessments (Loacker, 2000) and independent research findings on elements of self-assessment that were most often associated with effective five-year alumna performance (Mentkowski & Associates, 2000; Rogers & Mentkowski, 2004). This method provided a way to ground a criterion-based description of performance with estimates of inter-rater reliability. The complementary methods supported a triangulated and well-grounded description of the student teaching performances. As a result, the report has supported accountability of the teacher education department to external publics (including a site visit from the U.S. Department of Education for the 2000 National Award for Effective Teacher Preparation) and informed ongoing improvements in the assessment.

Criteria for Program, Curriculum, and Institution-Wide Assessment

The guidelines discussed above broadly describe assessment processes that we have found increase the meaningful use of program and institutional assessment to improve student learning. Program assessment at Alverno College, as at other institutions, occurs in the context of the larger institutional mission and the characteristics of its particular curriculum and student population. Faculty and staff at other institutions can use Alverno's program assessment examples to imagine their own new practices, but they also may find barriers in adapting specific examples when curriculum theory and educational cultures differ, and when there are different levels of faculty experience in defining and assessing for individual student learning outcomes across a program. We have found, however, that the fundamental commonality that enables us to have a productive conversation across differing practices and contexts is an institutional commitment to focusing on student learning. But what are the characteristics of a learning-centered institution?

Between 1999 and 2002, representatives from Alverno College and twenty-five other institutions collaborated on a project to describe the operation of learning-centered institutions in higher education. From the consortium's studies, learning-centered institutions had four distinguishing characteristics. They were committed to (1) achieving clarity about learning outcomes, (2) coordinating teaching and assessment to promote student learning, (3) aligning structures and resources to serve student learning, and (4) working continuously to improve the environment for learning (Doherty, Riordan, & Roth, 2002).

In this context, the definition of program and institutional assessment shared by the Student Learning Initiative may function as broad, generalizable criteria that learning-centered institutions can use to plan, evaluate, and study their assessment programs. As criteria, or benchmarks, the elements of program, curriculum, and institution-wide assessment from the Student Learning Initiative focus on studying student learning and support managing resources toward high levels of learning outcomes. Program assessment is also built on standards-based, analytic comparisons as a primary evidentiary base for judgments about curriculum and educational practices. And, most important, public dialogue about learning and achievement becomes a critical part of program improvement plans.

Concluding Observations

Alverno College's educational practices have developed from a central concern about student learning, integrating perspectives on educational inquiry, and the discourse of educators. It is also a relatively small undergraduate campus with a well-articulated teaching mission, serving women from diverse backgrounds. The guidelines and particular strategies discussed above have been drawn from that context, and this may have significance for their use elsewhere, even though we have found some broad agreement among learning-centered institutions.

Assessment processes conducted at the level of individual programs or the institution can be seen as inquiries into student learning and performance in relation to standards, criteria, and educational practices drawn from the program, accrediting bodies, and learned societies in the field. When they are conducted collaboratively by faculty and staff, the learning is shared among the educators for program planning and development and provides evidence-based judgments of value and worth for broader accountability. In comparison with some other perspectives on program evaluation, there is a clear effort in some practices, like ours, to engage in a collaborative process in which the judgments, interpretation of findings, and implications for future use are shared and integrated into the conduct of the study. In addition, however, our understanding of program assessment is fundamentally grounded in the idea of inquiring into the nature of student learning, how and why it happens, and for whom. For us, program assessment is closely tied to the educational task of inquiring into curriculum as a dynamic process with interactive elements (Mentkowski & Associates, 2000). We conclude with five recommendations for a community of scholarship, whether at the level of the program or the institution, that frame the task of making a learning-centered curriculum the lifeblood of program assessment.

Build a community of scholarship and practice in which program review and assessment have an organic role and inform educational practice and decisions. The work on faculty learning communities at Miami University of Ohio has provided some additional examples of how such efforts can evolve (Center for the Enhancement of Learning and Teaching, n.d.; Cox & Richlin, 2004).

Promote the scholarship of learning and teaching. A conscious approach to this dimension of scholarship plays an important role in conceptualizing the educational outcomes of program and institutional assessment (Banta & Associates, 2002; Mentkowski & Loacker, 2002). In particular, this scholarship can provide some basis for expanding the inquiry dimensions of program review and assessment (Weimer, 2001). This means infusing empirical study of student learning outcomes into pedagogical, curriculum, and program planning and decisions (Kreber, 2001; McAlpine & Weston, 2000; Saroyan, Amundsen, & Li, 1997).

Make use of the discourse opportunities on campus. The role of discourse or dialogue runs throughout the elements, guidelines, criteria, and examples discussed here. It represents a unique way in which a range of individuals—students, faculty, board members, legislators, and the public—participate in education (Huber, 1999). Understanding how different discourse communities develop and operate is an important step toward understanding how the conduct and outcomes of program and institutional assessments are taken up in educational practice.

Address the alignment of governance, curriculum, teaching practices, and commitment to student learning in the campus culture. For example, how do promotion and tenure processes recognize faculty efforts in program review and the application of policy results? Many colleges and universities have addressed this in their promotion and tenure criteria, but it remains an area of concern (see Hutchings, 2001; Mentkowski & Associates, 2000, pp. 355–358).

Consider the infrastructure by which assessment practices are implemented. A system of assessment that functions at the levels of individual student, program, curriculum, and institution requires an infrastructure that will sustain administrative practices and curriculum linkages, such as leadership, reporting, budgets, training, and support (see California State University, Bakersfield, 2001; California State University, San Jose, n.d.).

SAMPLE META-ASSESSMENT RUBRICS

Higher Learning Commission

See http://www.ncahigherlearningcommission.org

North Carolina State University

See http://www.ncsu.edu/assessment/evaluation/meta_analysis_rubric.pdf

Texas A&M University

See http://assessment.tamu.edu

REFERENCES

Accreditation Board for Engineering and Technology, Inc. (ABET). (2004). *Guidelines to institutions, team chairs and program evaluators on interpreting and meeting the standards set forth in criterion 3 of the engineering accreditation criteria.* Retrieved July 3, 2005, from http://www.abet.org/documents/eac/Criterion3 WhitePaper3-17-04.pdf

Allen, J., & Bresciani, M. J. (2003, January/February). Public institutions, public challenges: On the transparency of assessment results. *Change Magazine, 35*(1), 14–16.

Alverno College Faculty. (1994). *Student assessment-as-learning at Alverno College.* Milwaukee, WI: Alverno College Institute.

Alverno College Office of Educational Research and Evaluation. (2000). *The student teaching portfolios: An interim evaluation.* Milwaukee, WI: Alverno College Institute.

Alverno College Philosophy Faculty. (2003). *Ability-based learning program: The philosophy major* [brochure]. Milwaukee, WI: Alverno College Institute.

American Association of Higher Education. (1994). *Nine principles of good practice for assessing student learning.* Retrieved July 7, 2005, from http://www.aahe.org/ assessment/principl.html

American Association of University Professors. (1970). *1940 Statement of principles on academic freedom and tenure with 1970 interpretive comments.* Retrieved July 7, 2005, from http://www.aaup.org/statements/Redbook/1940stat.htm

Anderson, J. A., Maki, P., & Bresciani, M. J. (2001, July). *Expanding faculty involvement in assessment-based undergraduate academic program review: A case study.* Presentation at the American Association of Higher Education Assessment Conference, Boston.

Banta, T. W., & Associates. (2002). *Building a scholarship of assessment.* San Francisco: Jossey-Bass.

Bresciani, M. J. (2003, October). Expert Driven Assessment: Making It Meaningful to Decision Makers. *ECAR Research Bulletin, 21.* Boulder, CO: EDUCAUSE.

Bresciani, M. J. (2005, July). Small world does not mean small view. *Higher Education Digest.* Retrieved from http://www.internetviz-newsletters.com/datatele _article00042267.cfm?x = b11,0

Bresciani, M. J. (in press). *Exploring the epistemology of outcomes-based assessment.*

Bresciani, M. J., & Allen, J. (2004, September 7). If you build it: Assessment of student learning versus performance indicators. National Association for Student Personnel Administrators, Inc. Net Results E-Zine. Retrieved from http://www .naspa.org/membership/mem/nr/article.

Bresciani, M. J., Fry, D., & Remlinger, K. (in press). *Reasons faculty and administrators do not engage in outcomes-based assessment.*

Bresciani, M. J., Jenefsky, C., & Wolff, R. (in press). *Promoting the individual commodity of the faculty member: Where is the role of collaboration?*

Bresciani, M. J., Zelna, C. L., & Anderson, J. A. (2004). *Assessing student learning and development. A handbook for practitioners.* Washington, DC: National Association of Student Personnel Administrators.

California State University, Bakersfield. (2001, August). *Infrastructure to support assessment–CSUB.* Retrieved February 18, 2005, from http://www.csub.edu/assess mentcenter/infrastructure.htx

California State University, San Jose. (n.d.). *Assessment at SJSU undergraduate studies.* Retrieved February 18, 2005, from http://www2.sjsu.edu/ugs/assessment/as- sjsu.html

Carroll, Martin. (2005, May 29). A critical analysis of transnational education from a cultural relativist perspective. Keynote address at the Association of Institutional Research National Conference, San Diego, CA.

Center for the Enhancement of Learning and Teaching. (n.d.). *General information about faculty learning communities.* Retrieved February 18, 2005, from http:// www.units.muohio.edu/celt/communities.shtml

Council of Regional Accrediting Commissions (CRAC). (2003). *Regional accreditation and student learning: Principles of good practices.* Washington, DC: CRAC.

Covey, S. R. (1989). *The seven habits of highly effective people.* New York: Simon & Schuster.

Cox, M. D., & Richlin, L. (Eds.). (2004). *Building faculty learning communities.* New Directions for Teaching and Learning, No. 97. San Francisco: Jossey-Bass.

Dale, B., & Bunney, H. (1999). *Total quality management blueprint.* Malden, MA: Blackwell Publishing.

Design-Based Research Collective. (2003). Design-based research: An emerging paradigm for educational inquiry. *Educational Researcher, 32*(1), 5–8.

Diamond, R. M. (1998). *Designing & assessing courses & curricula: A practical guide.* San Francisco: Jossey-Bass.

Doherty, A., Riordan, T., & Roth, J. (2002). *Student learning: A central focus for institutions of higher education.* Milwaukee, WI: Alverno College Institute.

Eckel, P., Green, M., & Hill, B. (2001). *On change V—Riding the waves of change: Insights from transforming institutions.* Washington DC: American Council on Education.

Eder, D. J. (1999). *Installing authentic assessment: Putting assessment in its place.* Retrieved July 2, 2005, from http://www.siue.edu/~deder/assess/denvero.html

Engelmann, D. (2005). Teaching students to practice philosophy. In T. Riordan & J. Roth (Eds.), *Disciplines as frameworks for student learning: Teaching the practice of the disciplines* (pp. 39–58). Sterling, VA: Stylus Publishing, LLC.

Ewell, P. T. (1997a). From the states: Putting it all on the line—South Carolina's performance funding initiative. *Assessment Update, 9*(1), 9, 11.

Ewell, P. T. (1997b). Identifying indicators of curricular quality. In G. J. Gaff, L. J. Ratcliff, & Associates (Eds.), *Handbook of the undergraduate curriculum: A comprehensive guide to purposes, structures, practices, and change.* San Francisco: Jossey-Bass.

Ewell, P. T. (2002). An emerging scholarship: A brief history of assessment. In Banta & Associates, *Building a scholarship of assessment* (pp. 3–25). San Francisco: Jossey Bass.

Ewell, P. T. (2003, November). *Specific roles of assessment within this larger vision.* Presentation at the Assessment Institute at Indiana University–Purdue University Indianapolis, Indianapolis, IN.

Ewell, P. T., & Jones, D. P. (1996). *Indicators of good practice in undergraduate education. A handbook for development and implementation.* Boulder, CO: National Center for Higher Education Management Systems.

Frazier, A., & Frazier, M. A. (1997). A roadmap for quality transformation in education. Boca Raton, FL: CRC Press.

Goodchild, L. F., & Wechsler, H. S. (1989). *The history of higher education: Association of the Study of Higher Education reader.* Boston: Glenn Press.

Haworth, J. G., & Conrad, C. F. (1997). *Emblems of quality in higher education: Developing and sustaining high-quality programs.* Boston: Allyn & Bacon.

Herdegen, R. T. (2002, September). *Primary trait analysis for senior theses and research projects in a capstone course.* Paper presented at Measuring Up: Best Practices in Assessment in Psychology Programs, Atlanta, GA.

Herdegen, R. T. (2004, July). *Primary trait analysis for research reports in a capstone course.* Paper presented at the Annual Meeting of the American Psychological Association, Honolulu, HI.

Hernon, P. & Dugan, R. (2004). *Outcomes assessment in higher education: Views and perspectives.* Westport, CT: Libraries Unlimited.

Huba, Mary E., & Freed, Jann E. (2000). *Learner-centered assessment on college campuses/Shifting the focus from teaching to learning.* Needham Heights, MA: Allyn & Bacon.

Huber, M. T. (1999, March). *Developing discourse communities around the scholarship of teaching.* Presentation at the Colloquium on Campus Conversations, American Association for Higher Education, Washington, DC.

Hutchings, P. (2001). *Opening lines: Approaches to the scholarship of teaching and learning.* Menlo Park, CA: Carnegie Publications.

Johnstone, D. (2005, July/August). A competency alternative: Western Governors University. *Change, 37*(4), 19–23.

Kreber, C. (Ed.). (2001). *Scholarship revisited: Perspectives on the scholarship of teaching.* New Directions for Teaching and Learning, No. 86. San Francisco: Jossey-Bass.

Lee, V. S. (Ed.). (2004). *Teaching and learning through inquiry: A guidebook for institutions and instructors.* Sterling, VA: Stylus Publishing, LLC.

Loacker, G. (Ed.). (2000). *Self-assessment at Alverno College.* Milwaukee, WI: Alverno College Institute.

Loacker, G., & Mentkowski, M. (1993). Creating a culture where assessment improves learning. In T. W. Banta & Associates, *Making a difference: Outcomes of a decade of assessment in higher education* (pp. 5–24). San Francisco: Jossey-Bass.

Lopez, C. (1997). *Opportunities for improvement. Advice from consultant-evaluators on assessing student learning. Evidence of strong institutional support for assessing student learning.* Retrieved July 1, 2003, from http://www.ncahigherlearningcommission.org/resources/assessment/index.html

Lopez, C. (2002). Assessment of student learning. Challenges and strategies. *The Journal of Academic Librarianship, 28*(6), 356–367.

Lusthaus, C., Adrien, M-H, Anderson, G., & Carden, F. (1999). *Enhancing organizational performance.* Sterling, VA: Stylus Publishing, LLC.

Maki, P. (2004). *Assessing for student learning: Building a sustainable commitment across the institution.* Sterling, VA: Stylus Publishing, LLC.

Maki, P., & Bresciani, M. J. (2002, July). *Integrating student outcomes assessment into a university's culture.* Presentation at the American Association of Higher Education Faculty Forum on Roles and Rewards Conference, Phoenix, AZ.

McAlpine, L., & Weston, C. (2000). Reflection: Issues related to improving professors' teaching and students' learning. *Instructional Science, 28,* 363–385.

Mentkowski, M. (1991). Creating a context where institutional assessment yields educational improvement. *Journal of General Education, 40,* 255–283. (Reprinted in 1994 in J. S. Stark & A. Thomas [Eds.], *Assessment & program evaluation* [ASHE Reader Series; pp. 251–268]. Needham Heights, MA: Simon & Schuster Custom Publishing.)

Mentkowski, M. (1998). Higher education assessment and national goals for education: Issues, assumptions, and principles. In N. M. Lambert & B. L. McCombs (Eds.), *How students learn: Reforming schools through learner-centered education* (pp. 269–310). Washington, DC: American Psychological Association.

Mentkowski, M. (in press). Grounding student assessment in learning principles: Adaptable elements of the Alverno experience. In G. Gibbs, K. Clegg, & C. Bryan (Eds.), *Innovating in assessment.* London, UK: RoutledgeFalmer.

Mentkowski, M., & Associates. (2000). *Learning that lasts: Integrating learning, development, and performance in college and beyond.* San Francisco: Jossey-Bass.

Mentkowski, M., & Loacker, G. (1985). Assessing and validating the outcomes of college. In P. T. Ewell (Ed.), *Assessing educational outcomes.* New Directions for Institutional Research, No. 47 (pp. 47–64). San Francisco: Jossey-Bass.

Mentkowski, M., & Loacker, G. (2002). Enacting a collaborative scholarship of assessment. In T. W. Banta & Associates, *Building a scholarship of assessment* (pp. 82–99). San Francisco: Jossey-Bass.

Michelson, E., & Mandel, A. (Eds.). (2004). *Portfolio development and the assessment of prior learning.* Sterling, VA: Stylus Publishing, LLC.

NAFSA. (2004). *Survey of foreign students and scholar enrollment and visa trends for fall 2004.* Washington, DC: Author.

National Council for Accreditation of Teacher Education. (2002). *Professional standards for the accreditation of schools, colleges, and departments of education.* Washington, DC: Author.

Nichols, J. O. (2002). *A practitioner's handbook for institutional effectiveness and student outcomes assessment implementation* (3rd ed.). New York: Agathon Press.

North Carolina State's Committee on Undergraduate Program Review. *Conceptual understanding and common language for assessment.* Retrieved May 29, 2004, from http://www.North Carolina StateUniversity.edu/provost/governance/Ad_hoc/CUPR/retreats/concepts.html

Palomba, C. A., & Banta, T. W. (1999). *Assessment essentials. Planning, implementing, and improving assessment in higher education.* San Francisco: Jossey-Bass.

Papert, S. (1991). *Situating contructionism.* In S. Papert & I. Harel (Eds.), *Constructionism* (pp. 1–5). Cambridge, MA: MIT Press.

Pike, G. R. (2001). Assessment measures. *Assessment Update, 13*(1), 8.8. San Francisco: Jossey-Bass.

Rickards, W. H., Rogers, G. P., & Lake, K. (2004, April). *Evaluating teacher preparation programs: Using historical perspectives on evaluation studies and curriculum development.* Paper presented at the annual meeting of the American Educational Research Association, San Diego, CA.

Riordan, T., & Roth, J. (Eds.). (2005). *Disciplines as frameworks for student learning: Teaching the practice of the disciplines.* Sterling, VA: Stylus Publishing, LLC.

Rodrigues, R. (2002, September). *Want campus buy-in for your assessment efforts? Find out what's important to your faculty members and involve them throughout the process.* Retrieved September 3, 2002, from http://aahebulletin.com/member/articles/2002-10-feature02_1.asp

Rogers, G., & Mentkowski, M. (2004). Abilities that distinguish the effectiveness of five-year alumna performance across work, family, and civic roles: A higher education validation. *Higher Education Research & Development, 23*(3), 347–374.

Saroyan, A., Amundsen, C., & Li, C. (1997). Incorporating theories of teacher growth and adult education in a faculty development program. In D. DeZure (Ed.), *To improve the academy* (pp. 93–116). Fort Collins, CO: POD Network.

Senge, P. M. (1990). *The fifth discipline: The art and practice of the learning organization*. New York: Bantam Doubleday Dale Publishing Group.

Southern Association of Colleges and Schools (SACS). (2002). Accreditation Core Requirement 2.7.2.

Steele, J. (1989). Evaluating college programs using measures of student achievement and growth. *Educational Evaluation and Policy Analysis, 11,* 357–375.

Steele, J. M., & Lutz, D. A. (1995, June). *Report of ACT's research on postsecondary assessment needs.* Iowa City, IA: College Level Assessment & Survey Services, ACT.

Stevens, D. D., & Levi, A. J. (2004). *Introduction to rubrics: An assessment tool to save grading time, convey effective feedback and promote student learning.* Sterling, VA: Stylus Publishing, LLC.

Strauss, A., & Corbin, J. (1990). *Basics of qualitative research: Grounded theory procedures and techniques.* Newbury Park, CA: Sage.

Suskie, L. (2001). *Assessment to promote deep learning.* Sterling VA: Stylus Publishing, LLC.

Suskie, L. (2004). *Assessing student learning: A common sense guide.* Bolton, MA: Anker Publishing Company.

Tanner, D. E. (2001). *Assessing academic achievement.* Needham Heights, MA: Allyn & Bacon.

Torres, R. T., Preskill, H. S., & Piontek, M. E. (1996). *Evaluation strategies for communicating and reporting: Enhancing learning in organizations.* Thousand Oaks, CA: Sage.

Upcraft, M. L., & Schuh, J. H. (1996). *Assessment in student affairs: A guide for practitioners.* San Francisco: Jossey-Bass.

Weimer, M. (2001). Learning more from the wisdom of practice. In C. Kreber (Ed.), *Scholarship revisited: Perspectives on the scholarship of teaching* (pp. 45–56). New Directions for Teaching and Learning, No. 86. San Francisco: Jossey-Bass.

Wellman, J. (2005). The student credit hour: Counting what counts? *Change, 37*(4), 19–23.

Wergin, J. F. (1999, December). Evaluating department achievements: Consequences for the work of faculty. *AAHE Bulletin,* 1–4. Retrieved April 27, 2006 from http://www.niagara.edu/pol/images/Evaluating%20Departmental%20(AAHE).pdf

Wergin, J. F., & Swigen, J. N. (2000). *Departmental assessment. How some campuses are effectively evaluating the collective work of faculty.* Sterling, VA: Stylus Publishing, LLC.

Zeichner, K. (2000). Ability-based teacher education: Elementary teacher education at Alverno College. In L. Darling-Hammond (Ed.), *Studies of excellence in teacher education: Preparation in the undergraduate years* (pp. 1–66). Washington, DC: American Association of Colleges for Teacher Education.

ABOUT THE AUTHOR

Dr. Marilee J. Bresciani, associate professor for postsecondary education at San Diego State University, has held faculty and higher education administration positions for more than nineteen years. In those positions, she has conducted enrollment management research, quantitative and qualitative institutional research, course-embedded assessment, and academic and administrative program assessment. As assistant vice president for institutional assessment at Texas A&M University (TAMU) and as director of assessment at North Carolina State University, Dr. Bresciani enjoyed assisting units and departments campuswide in developing their assessment plans, identifying and developing assessment tools and methods, and using their data for continuous improvement of student learning and development. At TAMU, she coordinated university processes for assessment of programs and student learning and development and effective support for embedding those processes in faculty and staff's day-to-day work. In collaboration with others, Dr. Bresciani conducts outcomes assessment for specific programs and courses as well.

Dr. Bresciani has been invited to present assessment workshops nationally and internationally, has a number of invited publications, is the leading author of a book on assessing student learning and development, and is writing another book on general education assessment. Dr. Bresciani has developed and delivered several courses on assessment of student learning and serves on the editorial board of the *NASPA Journal*. She is a reviewer for the Australian Quality Assurance Agency and a managing partner in an international assessment and enrollment management consulting firm.

Dr. Bresciani earned a Ph.D. in administration, curriculum, and instruction from the University of Nebraska and a master of arts in teaching from Hastings College.